A Frantic A
Theatre Royal Ply
co-produced wit

I THINK WE ARE ALONE

SALLY ABBOTT

This production of *I Think We Are Alone* was
first performed on 3 February 2020 at
Theatre Royal Plymouth, before touring the UK

Photography © Tristram Kenton

CREATIVE TEAM

Writer	Sally Abbott
Co-directed	Kathy Burke
	Scott Graham
Set and Costume Design	Morgan Large
Lighting Design	Paul Keogan
Sound Design	Ella Wahlström
Associate Director	Jessica Williams
Producer	Peter Holland
Production Manager	Hugh Borthwick
Costume Supervisor	Delia Lancaster
Relighter	Matt Whale
Sound Associate	Mike Winship
Set Construction	Clockwork Scenery
Production Electrian	John Mann
Programmer	Jen Watson
Film	TeaFilms
	Michael Lynch

COMPANY

Josie	Chizzy Akudolu
Ange	Charlotte Bate
Clare	Polly Frame
Manny	Caleb Roberts
Bex	Simone Saunders
Graham	Andrew Turner
Grandad	Tarinn Callender
Company Stage Manager	Candice Wilson
Deputy Stage Manager	Liz Isaac
Assistant Stage Manager	Stefania Procter

FOR FRANTIC ASSEMBLY

Artistic Director	Scott Graham
Executive Director	Kerry Whelan
Producer	Peter Holland
General Manager	Angie Fullman
Head of Learning and Participation	Marilyn Rice
Learning and Participation Coordinator	Maya Pindar
Learn and Train Project Manager	Alisha Artry
Administrator	Vicky Olusanya
Associate Director, Learn & Train	Simon Pittman
Public Relations	Kate Hassell and Charlotte Winstone for Cornershop PR
Marketing and Sales	Natalie Yalden, Alex Ollington and Aimee White for JHI Marketing
Trustees	Sian Alexander (Chair to 1st March 2020)
	Mark Hawes (Chair Elect)
	Matthew Hunnybun
	Amit Kataria
	Tina Kokkinos
	Matthew Littleford
	Sally Noonan
	Joanna Read

FRANTIC ASSEMBLY

From a reckless leap into the unknown 25 years ago, Frantic Assembly has developed into one of the UK's most successful and best loved theatre companies.

Our ambition is that we continue to learn, and remain committed to making brave and bold theatre. At times it is physically dynamic and brutal. At others it's proudly tender and fragile.

But Frantic Assembly has always been about more than just the work on stage. It is about the ethos of collaboration, of empowerment, of that constant desire to improve. It is about telling stories in a voice we don't always hear and about finding talent in places we don't always look.

Led by Artistic Director and co-founder Scott Graham, our past productions include *The Unreturning*, *Fatherland*, *Things I Know To Be True*, *Othello*, *Beautiful Burnout*, *Lovesong*, *Stockholm* and *The Believers* and we have commissioned and collaborated with writers such as Anna Jordan, Simon Stephens, Andrew Bovell, Mark Ravenhill, Abi Morgan and Bryony Lavery.

Our distinct creative approach has influenced contemporary theatre-making and foregrounded the use of movement directors and choreographers in new dramatic works. It has inspired writers to embrace new creative processes and opened up actors and dancers to new techniques. This is a matter of great pride as we continue to do something different and to do it differently.

We also collaborate on other productions and provide the movement direction on the award-winning National Theatre of Great Britain production *The Curious Incident of the Dog in the Night-time* as well as for other projects such as the BAFTA nominated British/American TV series *Humans* (AMC, Channel 4 & Kudos).

We tour extensively across the UK and have worked in over 40 countries world-wide collaborating with some of today's most inspiring artists.

Frantic Assembly is studied as a leading contemporary theatre practitioner on five British and International academic syllabuses and the Frantic Method is taught around the world by our practitioners.

Our flagship programme, Ignition, is an innovative, free vocational training programme for young people aged 16 – 24, particularly targeting those with little or no previous experience of, or access to, the arts. Ignition has been unlocking creative potential in young people across the UK for over 12 years and aims to make the future of British theatre better, fairer and more inclusive.

Supported using public funding by
**ARTS COUNCIL
ENGLAND**

 Theatre
Royal
Plymouth

Theatre Royal Plymouth is a registered charity providing art, education and community engagement throughout Plymouth and the wider region. We engage and inspire many communities through performing arts and we aim to touch the lives and interests of people from all backgrounds. We do this by creating and presenting a breadth of shows on a range of scales, with our extensive creative engagement programmes, by embracing the vitality of new talent and supporting emerging and established artists, and by collaborating with a range of partners to provide dynamic cultural leadership for the city of Plymouth.

Recent productions and co-productions include *God Of Chaos* by Phil Porter, *The Kneebone Cadillac* by Carl Grose, *You Stupid Darkness!* by Sam Steiner (with Paines Plough), *The Unreturning* by Anna Jordan (with Frantic Assembly), *One Under* by Winsome Pinnock (with Graeae), *The Strange Tale of Charlie Chaplin and Stan Laurel* (with Told by an Idiot).

TRP has a strong track record of presenting and producing international work from companies and artists including Ontroerend Goed, Big In Belgium at the Edinburgh Festival Fringe, Robert Lepage and the late Yukio Ninagawa. In March 2019 TRP unveiled Messenger, the UK's largest bronze sculpture created by the artist Joseph Hillier.

Almost one million people annually engage with Curve through performances and projects at our home in Leicester, across the UK and internationally. Under the leadership of Chief Executive Chris Stafford and Artistic Director Nikolai Foster, Curve has developed a reputation for producing, programming and touring a bold and diverse programme of musicals, plays, new work, dance and opera. All of this presented alongside a dynamic mix of community engagement, artist development and learning programmes, which firmly places audiences, artists and communities at the heart of everything we do.

In 2019, three Curve originated productions played in London's West End; *On Your Feet!* (London Coliseum), Sue Townsend's *The Secret Diary of Adrian Mole Aged 13¾ – The Musical* (The Ambassadors Theatre) and *White Christmas* (Dominion Theatre).

Recent Made at Curve productions include Giles Andreae and Guy Parker Rees' *Giraffes Can't Dance*, *West Side Story*, Hanif Kureishi's *My Beautiful Laundrette* (co-produced with Belgrade Theatre Coventry, Everyman Theatre Cheltenham and Leeds Playhouse), John Osborne's *The Entertainer* (co-produced with Anthology Theatre and Simon Friend), A Curve Young Company and Community production of Bollywood Jane, a new UK tour of Jim Jacobs & Warren Casey's *Grease*, Alice Walker's Tony award-winning musical *The Color Purple* (co-produced with Birmingham Hippodrome), Gloria and Emilio Estefan's *On Your Feet!*, Irving Berlin's *White Christmas*, Dr. Seuss's *The Cat in the Hat* (and UK tour) the world-premiere of Dougal Irvine's adaptation of Riaz Khan's *Memoirs of an Asian Football Casual*, the Curve Young Company and Community production of Joseph Stein's *Fiddler on the Roof*, the world première production of *An Officer and a Gentleman* (& on national tour), Leslie Bricusse's *Scrooge*, the world première of Amana Fontanella Khan's *Pink Sari Revolution*, adapted by Purva Naresh (with Belgrade Theatre Coventry, English Touring Theatre and West Yorkshire Playhouse, Leeds); a major revival of Andrew Lloyd Webber's *Sunset Boulevard* (and UK tour), Winner – Best Musical, Manchester Theatre Awards and Best Regional Production, WhatsOnStage Awards; the world premiere of Ravi Shankar's opera *Sukanya* (co-produced with the Royal Opera House & London Philharmonic Orchestra) and the 50th anniversary production of Joe Orton's *What the Butler Saw* (with Theatre Royal Bath).

Curve is supported by Arts Council England and Leicester City Council.

Supported using public funding by
ARTS COUNCIL ENGLAND

CREATIVE TEAM BIOGRAPHIES

SALLY ABBOTT (WRITER)

Sally's previous theatre credits include: *Borough Market*, *One Saturday* co-written with Michael Begley which won the Triforce Monologue Slam; *Martha Loves Michael* again co-written with Michael Begley for their company Ruffian Productions/The Hat Factory, Cambridge; and *Not Mad*, *Doors*, *Freedom is Orange* and *Tales From an Emerald City* for English Touring Theatre's Youth Theatre. For TV, she created the award-winning BBC drama *The Coroner* which ran for two series on BBC1 and is shown all over the world. Other tv credits include *Vera*, *Death in Paradise*, *Holby*, *Eastenders* and *Casualty*. She trained on Acting Out at Liverpool's Hope Street Project and on the prestigious BBC Drama Writers Academy. She is proud to be a patron of Next Generation Youth Theatre in Luton.

KATHY BURKE (CO-DIRECTOR)

Kathy Burke has worked extensively as director, actor and writer enjoying considerable success in each of the disciplines.

Theatre directing includes: *Lady Windemere's Fan* (Vaudeville Theatre), *The Retreat* by Sam Bain (Park Theatre), *Once a Catholic* by Mary O'Malley (Kiln Theatre), *Smaller* by Carmel Morgan (Lyric Theatre, London), *The God of Hell* by Sam Shepard (Donmar Warehouse), *Blue/Orange* by Joe Penhall (Sheffield Crucible and tour), *Love Me Tonight* by Nick Stafford (Hampstead Theatre), *The Quare Fellow* by Brendan Behan (Oxford Stage Company), *Born Bad* by Debbie Tucker Green (Hampstead Theatre), *Kosher Harry* by Nick Grosso (Royal Court Theatre), *Betty* by Karen McLachlan (Vaudeville Theatre), *Out in the Open* by Jonathan Harvey (Hampstead Theatre) and *Mr Thomas* for the Old Red Lion, which Kathy also wrote.

Kathy won Best Actress at Cannes (1997) and a BIFFA Award for *Nil By Mouth*; a British Comedy Award (2002) for *Gimme Gimme Gimme* and an RTS Award for *Mr Wroe's Virgins* (1994).

Recent film work includes: *Absolutely Fabulous the Movie*, *Pan*, *Tinker Tailor Soldier Spy*.

Kathy is well known for her TV work which includes: *Walking and Talking* which she wrote and acted in as 'the Nun', *Ab Fab*, *Gimme Gimme Gimme* and several series of *Harry Enfield and Chums* and the spin-off film *Kevin and Perry Go Large*.

Writing credits include the award winning stage play *Mr Thomas* which was later televised and a *Little Cracker* for Sky called *Better Than Christmas* which led to a spin off four part series called *Walking and Talking*.

Wanting to try new things, Kathy presented a documentary for Channel 4 *Kathy Burke's All Woman* which aired in 2019.

Upcoming work includes directing the transfer of the hit Edinburgh Festival show *#HonestAmy* which transfers to the Turbine Theatre, London in March 2020 and *The Cavalcaders* by Billy Roche which will play at The Boulevard Theatre from September 2020.

SCOTT GRAHAM (CO-DIRECTOR)

Scott is Artistic Director of Frantic Assembly, co-founding the company in 1994. He has received nominations for his work on *Beautiful Burnout* (Drama Desk Award, New York), *Curious Incident* (Olivier, Tony and Fred Astaire Awards). With Steven Hoggett he won the TMA Award (now UK Theatre Awards) for Best Direction for *Othello*. He has provided movement direction for shows at the Royal National Theatre, National Theatre Wales and Singapore Rep. He has developed and written extensively about The Frantic Method. His recent directing credits with Frantic Assembly include *Things I Know To Be True*, *Fatherland* and *Sometimes Thinking*. With Steven Hoggett, he has written *The Frantic Assembly Book of Devising Theatre* (Routledge).

MORGAN LARGE (DESIGNER)

West End credits include *Joseph and the Amazing Technicolor* Dreamcoat (London Palladium); *Cat on a Hot Tin Roof* (Novello Theatre); *The Last Tango* (Phoenix Theatre/UK Tour); *Forbidden Broadway* (Vaudeville Theatre/Menier Chocolate Factory); *Midnight Tango* (Phoenix Theatre/ Aldwych Theatre/UK Tours); *Dance 'til Dawn* (Aldwych Theatre/UK Tour); *Ruthless!* (Arts Theatre); *Flashdance* (Shaftesbury Theatre); *Sign of the Times* (Duchess Theatre) and *Footloose* (Playhouse Theatre/Novello Theatre/UK Tour/South Africa).

London credits include *Guys and Dolls* (Royal Albert Hall); *Violet*, *The Woman in White* and *Death Takes a Holiday* (Set Design, Charing Cross Theatre); *Spamilton* (Menier Chocolate Factory/US Tour) and *The Christmasaurus* (Hammersmith Apollo).

Other credits include *The Enemy of the People* and *Wonderland* (Nottingham Playhouse); *Othello* and *Lives in Art* (Sheffield Crucible); *Our New Girl* (Bush Theatre); *The Lady Vanishes* and *Rain Man* (Bill Kenwright Ltd); *Top Hat* (Set Design) and *Thoroughly Modern Millie* (Kilworth House); *George's Marvellous Medicine* (Leicester Curve/UK Tour); *Deathtrap* (Salisbury Playhouse/UK Tour); *Room on the Broom* (Lyric Theatre/Garrick Theatre/World Tour); and UK tours of *Rock of Ages*, *Fame!*, *Love Me Tender* and *Tango Moderno*.

International credits include *Tell Me on a Sunday* (Set Design, Majestic Theatre, Shanghai/RUG) and *The Life of the Party* (TheatreWorks, California/Menier Chocolate Factory).

Awards include UK Theatre Award for Best Design for Wonderland and Olivier Award for Best Revival of a Play for *Cat on a Hot Tin Roof*.

PAUL KEOGAN (LIGHTING DESIGN)

Previous designs include; *Plough and The Stars* (Lyric Hammersmith/ Abbey Theatre, Dublin); *Shirley Valentine*, *Double Cross* (Lyric Theatre, Belfast); *Blood in the Dirt*, *The Walworth Farce* (Landmark, Dublin); *Last Orders at the Dockside*, *Citysong*, (Abbey Theatre, Dublin); *Lady Windermere's Fan*, *De Profundis*, *Smaller* (London, West End); *Miracle on 42nd Street*, *A Streetcar Named Desire* (Liverpool Everyman & Playhouse); *Cyprus Avenue* (Abbey, Dublin/Royal Court), *Harvest* (Royal Court, London); *The Caretaker* (Bristol Old Vic); *Hamlet*, (Gate Theatre, Dublin); *Incantata*, (Galway International Festival); *Far Away* (Corcadorca, Cork);

The Gaul (Hull Truck Theatre); *Born Bad* (Hampstead Theatre, London); *Novecento* (Trafalgar Studios, London).

Opera and Dance designs include: *Marriage of Figaro* and *Aida* (Irish National Opera); *The Return of Ulysses* (Opera Collective, Ireland); *Falstaff* (Vienna Staatsoper); *Jenufa, La Bohème, Eugene Onegin, Idomeneo, Les Dialogues des Carmelites* (Grange Park Opera UK); *Powder Her Face* (Teatro Arriaga, Bilbao); *The Fairy Queen* (RIAM Dublin); *Maria de Buenos Aires* (Cork Opera House); *Wake* (Nationale Reisopera, Netherlands); *Lost* (Ballet Ireland); *Sama* and *Flight* (Rambert); *No Man's Land* (English National Ballet); *Cassandra, Hansel and Gretel* (Royal Ballet, UK).

ELLA WAHLSTRÖM (SOUND DESIGN)

Ella is an international Sound Designer. She was born in Finland and moved to London in 2010 to train at Rose Bruford College. Her recent sound design credits include: *Noises Off* (Garrick), *Peter Pan Goes Wrong* (Alexandra Palace, UK tour), *Jellyfish* (The National Theatre), *Sometimes Thinking* (National Theatre, River Stage) *Black&White* (SJACC, Kuwait), *Trying it On* (UK tour, RSC, Royal Court, Traverse), *Inside Bitch* (Royal Court), *The Life* (English Theatre Frankfurt). She's the sound designer of Esa-Pekka Salonen's Cello Concerto which premiered in Chicago in 2017 with Yo-Yo Ma as the soloist and the co-sound designer of Robert Wilson and Mikhail Baryshnikov's *Letter to a Man*.

JESSICA WILLIAMS (ASSOCIATE DIRECTOR)

Jess works as a Movement Director, Director and Performer, she trained at the London Contemporary Dance School and the Laban Centre. She has been a Frantic practitioner since 2012.

Jess was Associate Director for Frantic Assembly's *The Unreturning*. She toured the UK in *The Curious Incident of the Dog in the Night-Time* for the National Theatre and Frantic Assembly and has been Associate Movement Director for the USA, World Tour and West End productions of the same show. Jess also performed in *This Will All Be Gone* for Frantic Assembly.

In 2019 Jess co-directed the *Ignition for Women* pilot for Frantic and is very excited about the future of this project.

Recent credits as Movement Director include:
One Flew Over the Cuckoo's Nest (English Theatre Frankfurt); *Constellations*' (National Centre for Performing Arts, Mumbai); *UrineTown* and Flower Cutters (Perfect Pitch, UCLAN); *Tuck* and *A Good Clean Heart* (Neontopia, Wales Millennium Centre); *Merched Caerdydd* (Theatr Genedlaethol Cymru); *Wonderland* (Nottingham Playhouse - Associate movement director); *AWOL* (ThickSkin Theatre).

In 2019/2020 Jess performed in *Ocean at the End of the Lane* at the National Theatre.

WILL BURTON (CASTING DIRECTOR)

West End theatre includes: *Matilda* (Cambridge); *Heathers* (Haymarket); *Everybody's Talking About Jamie* (Apollo); *The Selfish Giant* (Vaudeville); *Ghost* (Piccadilly)

London theatre includes: *Be More Chill* (The Other Palace); *High Fidelity, Torch Song* (Turbine Theatre); *Ghost Quartet* (Boulevard Theatre); *Evita* (Barbican & Regent's Park); *Jesus Christ Superstar* (Barbican & Regent's Park); *Local Hero, Jekyll & Hyde, High Society* (Old Vic); *The View Upstairs* (Soho Theatre); *Leave To Remain, Bugsy Malone* (Lyric Hammersmith); *Fatherland* (Frantic Assembly); *Five Guys Named Moe* (Marble Arch); *The Wild Party, Heathers, Bonnie & Clyde, Starlight Express* (The Other Palace); *In the Heights* (Kings Cross Theatre); *Working, Xanadu, Carrie, Casa Valentina, Side Show* (Southwark Playhouse); *The Etienne Sisters* (Stratford East); *Paper Dolls* (Tricycle); *bare* (Union).

Regional theatre & tours includes: *Insane Animals* (HOME, Manchester); *I Think We Are Alone* (Frantic Assembly/UK Tour); *Priscilla Queen of the Desert* (UK tour); *Everybody's Talking About Jamie* (UK tour); *Local Hero* (Edinburgh Lyceum); *Kiss Me, Kate, The Wizard of Oz, Everybody's* Talking *About Jamie* (Sheffield Crucible); *Sweet Charity* (Nottingham Playhouse); *RENT 20th Anniversary* (UK Tour); *Miracle on 34th Street* (Liverpool Playhouse); *The Wizard of Oz* (Birmingham Rep); *The Assassination of Katie Hopkins* (Theatr Clwyd); *The Secret Diary of Adrian Mole 13¾* (Curve).

TV and film includes: *Mary Poppins Returns, Beauty & the Beast* (Disney); *The Voice, So You Think You Can Dance, Over The Rainbow* (BBC); *Superstar* (ITV).

Will is a full member of The Casting Directors Guild and is represented by Curtis Brown.

CAST BIOGRAPHIES

CHIZZY AKUDOLU (JOSIE)

Chizzy's theatre credits include *Edmond de Bergerac* (Birmingham Rep, UK Tour); *The Rec Room* (Triforce Promotions/Soho Theatre); *Script Slam* (Soho Theatre); *King of the Castle* (Tell Tarra); *The Vagina Monologues* (UK Tour/Mark Goucher Ltd); *Hells Fury* – rehearsed reading (Royal Court/Tell Tarra); *Mixt Nutz* (Guilded Balloon); *Soho Script Slam*, *Ready, Steady, Write, The Weave* (Soho Theatre); *Da Olympics 2012* – rehearsed reading, *Club V, The Best of Funny Black Women on the Edge* (Theatre Royal Stratford East); *Blaggers* (Aarawak Moon); *BBC Talent Urban Sketch Showcase* (BBC) and *Common Threads* (Gwent Theatre).

Her television credits include *Hetty Feather Christmas*, *Casualty*, *Death in Paradise*, *Shakespeare and Hathaway*, *Tracey Breaks the News*, *Holby City*, *Silent Witness*, *Mongrels*, *Twenty Twelve*, *Unzipped with Miranda Hart*, *Maynard* – rehearsed reading, *The Marc Wootton Project*, *Stupid*, *Eastenders*, *15 Storeys High* (BBC); *The Jewish Enquirer* (Magnet Films); *Sorry, I Didn't Know* (Triforce Creative Network/ITV); *Hood* (BBC Three); *Meet The Pranksters* (Gallowgate TV); *Campus* (Monkier Pictures/ Channel 4); *The Inbetweeners, series 3* (Bwark Productions); *The Increasingly Poor Decisions of Todd Margaret* (RDF Television); *Scoop, Scoop 2, Scoop 3* (CBBC); *Jinx* (Kindle Entertainment); *Team UK, The Complete Guide to Parenting, Green Wing* (Talkback); *Gigglebiz, Nuzzle & Scratch* (Cbeebies); *Dead Set* (Zeppotron); *Roman's Empire* (Tiger Aspect) and *Cul De Sac* (Picture Farm).

Chizzy's film credits include *County Lines* (Two Birds Entertainment/Loupe Films); *In the Loop* (BBC Films); *Dustbin Baby* (Kindle Entertainment); *The Most Unromantic Man in the World* (Burning Vision Entertainment); *Jack Brown & The Curse of the Crown* (Hot Gold Ltd); *Weave Wars* (short), *5 Minutes* (short); *Agent* (short); *Home Sweet Home* (short); *Jeans Tooth* (short); *Justanaxident* (short); *Child Accident Prevention Trust* (short); *Stretch Yer Tights* (short) (City Films); *Having More Sence* (short); *Miss Sparks* (Archistudio Films) and *Hood Documentary* (short).

Radio credits include: *Maynard* (BBC Radio 4); *Nathan Caton* (BBC Radio 4); *The Headset Set* (BBC Radio 4); *Carphone Warehouse* (Radioville) and *Sharp Cuts* (Choice FM).

CHARLOTTE BATE (ANGE)

Charlotte trained at The Guildhall School of Music and Drama.

Her theatre credits include *On The Other Hand We're Happy*, *Daughterhood and Dexter* and *Winter's Detective Agency* (Paines Plough/ Theatre Royal Stratford East), *Blackthorn* (West Yorkshire Playhouse), *The Rivals* (The Watermill Theatre), *King Lear* (The Orange Tree Theatre), *Watership Down* (The Watermill Theatre) and *Romeo and Juliet* (Sheffield Crucible).

Charlotte's television credits include *Casualty* (BBC), *White House Farm* (ITV) and *Philip K. Dick's Electric Dreams* (Channel 4).

POLLY FRAME (CLARE)

Polly trained at Bristol University.

Her theatre credits include *Solaris* (Edinburgh Lyceum/Lyric Hammersmith), *Sometimes Thinking* (Frantic Assembly), *After Edward* and *Edward II* (Globe Theatre), *Thick as Thieves* (Clean Break Theatre), *On the Exhale Fringe First Winner* (Traverse Theatre), *Jekyll & Hyde* (English Touring Consortium), *A Short History of Tractors in Ukrainian* (Hull Truck), *Dr Frankenstein* and *Hedda Gabler* (Northern Stage), *Henry V* (Regent's Park Open Air Theatre), *The Odyssey* (English Touring Theatre), *Mermaid* (Shared Experience), *Arcadia* (Tobacco Factory), *Twelfth Night* (Filter Theatre), *Pastoral* (Soho Theatre), *After Miss Julie* (Young Vic), *The Crossing 66 Books* (Bush Theatre), *The Comedy of Errors* (Stafford Shakespeare Festival), *Earthquakes in London* (RNT), *The Count of Monte Cristo* (West Yorkshire Playhouse), *Macbeth* (Chichester, West End & Broadway), *A Response to Twelfth Night* (Filter), *Cleansed* (Arcola).

Polly's television credits include *Doctors* (BBC), *Casualty* (BBC), *Man Down* (Channel 4), *The Tunnel* (Kudos Film & Canal), *Coronation Street* (ITV), *Holby City* (BBC), *The Curse of the Hope Diamond* (Blink Films), *Silent Witness* (BBC), *EastEnders* (BBC), *Bunny Town* (BBC 2 Thumbs Up/Disney), *Sea of Souls* (Carnival Films/BBC), *Accused* (BBC), *Life Begins* (ITV), *New Tricks* (Wall to Wall), *Meet the Magoons* (Channel 4), *The Giblets* (ITV), *Servants* (BBC).

Her film credits include *Macbeth* (Illuminations), *Half Light* (Half-Light Productions), *Duplicity* (Galleon Films).

CALEB ROBERT (MANNY)

Caleb's theatre credits include *She Ventures and He Wins* (The Young Vic), *Richard III* (Headlong), *Double Dealer* (Orange Tree), *King Lear* (West End/Chichester Festival).

His television credits include *A Very English Scandal* (BBC).

SIMONE SAUNDERS (BEX)

Simone's theatre credits include *Chicken Soup* (Sheffield Crucible), *Darkness Darkness* (Nottingham Playhouse); *Jane Eyre* (National Theatre and Bristol Old Vic); *American Trade*, *Morte D'Arthur*, *Romeo and Juliet*, *Hamlet*, *The Grain Store*, *The Winter's Tale*, *Julius Caesar* (Royal Shakespeare Company); *Carnival* (Talawa Theatre Company); *The Tempest* (Northern Broadsides); *The Red Ladies* (Clod Ensemble and National Theatre); *Double Take* (Nottingham Playhouse).

Her television credits include *Moving On* (BBC), *Clink* (Lime Pictures), *The Royals* (Lionsgate for E!); *Doctors* (BBC), *Casualty* (BBC).

ANDREW TURNER (GRAHAM)

Andrew's theatre credits include *Connection* (Harrogate), *Dancehall* (Cast Doncaster), *Cat in the Rain*, *Dumb Waiter* (Chief Theatre Company), *Twelfth Night* (Northampton Royal), *The White Album*, *Sam's Game*

(Nottingham Playhouse), *Fields of Gold* (Stephen Joseph Theatre), *The Dark* (Donmar) and *Bintou* (Arcola).

His television credits include *Father Brown* (BBC), *Mount Pleasant* (Sky), *The Musketeers* (BBC), *Coronation Street* (ITV), *Doctors* (BBC), *Bad Debt* (Peter Bullock Productions), *Holby City* (BBC), *Blue Murder* (Granada), *Casualty* (BBC), *Snuff Box* (BBC), *The Somme* (Darlow Smithson), *Waking the Dead* (BBC), and *Dalziel and Pascoe* (BBC).

Andrew's film credits include *Fantastic Beasts: The Crimes of Grindelwald* (Warner Bros) and *Is Anybody There?* (BBC Films)

I Think We Are Alone explores themes relating to loneliness, grief and abuse. If you have been affected by any of the issues raised in the play, we have a comprehensive guide of resources and contacts you may wish to consider reading. Please visit www.franticassembly.co.uk/dont-be-alone for more information.

DIRECTOR'S NOTE

This project began with a fascination about our shifting relationship with intimacy, loneliness and our desire for connection.

I wanted strong collaborators with distinct voices and I could not have wished for more in Sally Abbott and Kathy Burke. Despite our appreciation of each other's work, this collaboration was still a leap of faith. We had to find how to communicate. As ever, the best way to do that was to listen.

I remember a writer saying to me once that he thought the key to collaboration was never saying no. I know what he means. It is not about always saying yes but always leaving the space to be inspired and surprised by what your collaborators might bring to the moment. Otherwise, what is the point of having collaborators?

This project would not have happened without the collaboration. As an idea, it remained dormant and needed the fresh perspectives Sally and Kathy brought. The same with Morgan Large, Paul Keogan and Ella Wahlström. And they brought it with such generosity and humour, it made the process an absolute pleasure.

I know Kathy would also like to thank the performers and those actors who contributed to the development sessions. Their trust, energy and commitment is absolutely integral. Their work has shocked us, made us howl with laughter and made us cry. We are in awe and a little bit in love with them.

All projects are exhausting and we write this suitably exhausted but also exhilarated by the input of performers, designers and a wonderfully creative and supportive stage management team. Thank you, you glorious things!

Scott and Kathy

TOUR DATES

THEATRE ROYAL PLYMOUTH
03 – 8 Feb 2020
www.theatreroyal.com

LIVERPOOL PLAYHOUSE
11 – 15 Feb 2020
www.everymanplayhouse.com

KING'S THEATRE, EDINBURGH
17 – 21 Feb 2020
www.capitaltheatres.com

THEATRE ROYAL STRATFORD EAST
25 Feb – 21 Mar 2020
www.stratfordeast.com

CURVE THEATRE, LEICESTER
24 – 28 Mar 2020
www.curveonline.co.uk

NUFFIELD SOUTHAMPTON THEATRES
31 Mar – 4 Apr 2020
www.nstheatres.co.uk

YVONNE ARNAUD THEATRE, GUILDFORD
14 – 18 Apr 2020
www.yvonne-arnaud.co.uk

NORTHERN STAGE, NEWCASTLE
21-25 Apr 2020
www.northernstage.co.uk

BRISTOL OLD VIC
28 Apr – 02 May 2020
www.bristololdvic.org.uk

OXFORD PLAYHOUSE
04 – 09 May 2020
www.oxfordplayhouse.com

THE LOWRY, SALFORD
12 – 16 May 2020
www.thelowry.com

www.franticassembly.co.uk

THANKS

Abigail Parry
Amaka Okafor
Amy Morgan
Andrew Turner
Barnaby Taylor
Bella Rodrigues
Craig Stein
Daisy Maywood
Dame Sian Phillips
Ebony Molina
Eileen Walsh
Ella Burns
James Penford
Jess Alford
Jim Reardon
Joe Layton
Josie Walker
Karl Hyde
Kate Marlais
Laura Hopkins
Leila Crerar
Lily Simpkiss
Lindsey Coulson
Lucy Fawcett
Lucy Scriven
Maisie Brooker
Matthew Trevannion
Michael Begley
Molly Hughes
Perou
Polly Frame
Richard Smith
Seline Hizli
Sophie Melville
Tal Rosner
Theatre Royal Stratford East
Tige Burns
Vicky Manning
Bernard and Susan Abbott
Reiss Akhtar
Teresa Burns
Amanda Duke
Molly Hughes
Morgan Lloyd-Malcolm

CHAMPION

This year Frantic Assembly is celebrating its 25th Birthday. We are asking for your help to support the work we do by making a donation to our 25@25 fundraising appeal.

Since 1994 Frantic Assembly has been making exciting theatre; breaking down barriers to engagement and participation and providing opportunities for young people to discover and develop careers in the arts.

Our 25@25 appeal has a simple ambition; to raise £25,000 in our 25th year to help us continue creating thrilling theatre and vital opportunities to develop young talent.
You can do this by making a one-off donation or by setting up a regular monthly Direct Debit.

We also invite you to be a part of the Frantic journey by becoming a Frantic Champion. For an annual donation of £10 Champions will receive regular news updates and advance notice of shows and events. More than that though you'll be supporting our work – you'll be a Champion of the company and part of the world-wide Frantic family.

Please visit our website www.franticassembly.co.uk/support-us to find out how you can help support our work or contact Kerry Whelan, Executive Director at kerry@franticassembly.co.uk

Thank you.

Frantic Assembly is a Registered Charity (Reg No. 1113716)

Support Frantic Assembly by visiting our online shop.

Visit www.franticassembly.co.uk/shop for a full range of merchandise including play texts, clothing, water bottles, books and more.
All purchases help to fund our work both on and off stage.

Thank you.

I THINK WE ARE ALONE

Sally Abbott

For my sister, Vicky; my soul sister, Lucy;
For Michael, Ella and Tige, who always said I could do it.
And for Sarah.

Acknowledgements

Thanks to:

Bernard and Susan Abbott, Reiss Akhtar, Michael Begley, Maisie Brooker, Kathy Burke, Ella Burns, Teresa Burns, Tige Burns, Amanda Duke, Lucy Fawcett, Scott Graham, Peter Holland, Molly Hughes, Morgan Lloyd Malcolm, Vicky Manning, Jim Reardon, Lucy Scriven, Lily Simpkiss, Barnaby Taylor and the beautiful family that is Frantic Assembly.

S.A.

As Buddha once said: 'The secret of health for both mind and body is not to mourn for the past, not to worry about the future, not to anticipate troubles, but to live in the present moment wisely and earnestly.'

And, I'd like to add, if Buddha doesn't mind, to have a bloody good laugh along the way.

Sarah Reardon
(*1969–2010*)

4

Characters

CLARE, *thirty-seven, Clare without an 'i', works in HR, lives in an expensive flat in North London with Steve*

ANGE, *thirty-four, her sister, works at a hospice, lives alone in a co-op-owned studio flat*

JOSIE, *forty-eight to forty-nine, works on a garage reception, lives in a two-bed council flat in South London*

MANNY, *twenty-three, her son, state-educated in South London, now in his second year at Cambridge*

BEX, *thirty-eight, mother of a baby and a toddler, patient at Ange's hospice. Northern*

GRAHAM, *forty-one, a working-class, black-cab-driving, dad of two. Also Northern*

Dialogue in square brackets [ ] is not spoken out loud.

The Setting

London.

We inhabit the following worlds; the detail is for atmosphere and information, not a literal interpretation:

Clare's home – her bedroom – bed and wardrobe – and living room.

Ange's studio flat – living/sleeping area.

Woodside Hospice – Ange's work. Bright, daylight-filled open-plan areas for day-care patients. Private rooms with beds in for in-patients.

Josie's living room. Nothing is new. Every penny has been spent on Manny. A council flat on the first floor, off a high street in South London. A table, a hi-fi, a framed newspaper clipping of Manny and Josie. Several doors.

Fix-U-Fast Autos – Josie's work. The front desk of a garage, the same framed newspaper cutting of Manny and Josie.

Suki's – a nightclub – indie/disco/kitsch/fabulous/straight/queer.

The Butcher's Slab, a slightly pretentious Shoreditch bar.

A promontory on the South Bank, by the OXO Tower Wharf, the OXO Tower towering behind it.

A London park.

Westminster Bridge.

Graham's black cab and the London streets that he trawls as a cabby.

Graham's bedroom – a wardrobe.

King's Cross Station concourse.

The Timeframe

The play is spread across two different time periods – when Bex was alive and the present day, which stretches over several months.

Bex only appears in the past, apart from as a ghost with Graham (although we shouldn't realise that her character is a ghost). I've indicated each time as a flashback to ensure the logic is there, but the audience should feel it is concurrent.

This text went to press before the end of rehearsals and so may differ slightly from the play as performed.

JOSIE *enters, carries a large potted houseplant. Puts it down.*

JOSIE. I like animals more than people. Dogs are my thing. When you have a dog, well, for the first – maybe only time – you're given unconditional love.

It doesn't matter what mood you're in, they still love you. Dogs.

They love people who don't deserve to be loved. People who hit 'em and –

Ooh.

People who hurt animals. Don't get me [fucking] started.

See, people in general, I'm not a big fan.

We got Queenie from the rescue. Battersea Dogs Home. Me and my boy, Manny. Greyhound. Used to be a racer. The dog. Not my boy. She was in a bad way. Half-deaf, dodgy hip. The wind. Oh my God… She was put to sleep, ten weeks ago. I had to. It's fine, it's fine. It was for the best. Better two weeks too early, than a day too late. Sometimes, when you love someone, you have to do what's right for them, even if it hurts you. Queenie had dementia. She'd stopped sleeping. Didn't know where she was. Kept barking at rabbits. I live on the first floor. There were no rabbits.

She wasn't well. I knew what I was doing was right, didn't make it any easier. But I couldn't let her know I was scared cos then she'd sense it. She'd be scared. So, me and Manny pretended it was all okay. Just having a little cuddle. Last thing she did was lick some bacon off my fingers.

What a way to die. With the person you love and a little bit of bacon.

Picks up plant.

She's in here. That way she's still with me. I keep her near the window. The sun's rays coming in, it was her favourite place to sleep. With the sun on her back.

Hot dog.

It's too quiet now in the flat. Sometimes, I think I hear her breathing, the little rattle of her tags when she shakes herself. It's what I miss most. Her breathing.

ANGE. I think death is very frightening for people. The most frightening thing they can think of. But for some, it's a relief. They're ready. They're in so much pain, they're so tired. They want to go. Some just sleep into it, just disappear.

That's what I'd want. Something quick. I've thought about it a lot. How I want to die. Not an accident because. It's too messy. There'll be blame and other people involved.

That sounds very morbid. I'm not obsessed with death. I work in a hospice. It's busy. Never stops. Always full. Oversubscribed. Fifteen deaths a month minimum.

That's not my favourite thing about the job. People dying. Although it is a. This might sound weird but. It's a gift to be with someone when they die.

But once they've left. Once they're not suffering. Well, then you've got the ones who've been left behind and… If there's one thing I've learned, you've got to make your peace before it's too late. You've got to deal with your shit. This is your life. This one. It's not a practice one.

You get one life. One.

You don't want regrets. And you don't want to live your life thinking it's all about what happens on the other side cos, well. That's like buying a lottery ticket only, y'know, worse odds.

I work a lot with people who have faith. Staff. Patients. Volunteers. And some do have faith. But for some, it's just their get-out-of-jail-free card. It's why they volunteer – so God will look down and give them Brownie points.

But I don't think it works like that. I think God – if she exists
– would know exactly what people are like on the inside.
I reckon that's how it would work. Cos, I mean, take Jimmy
Savile. No matter how many marathons he ran, how much
money he raised, how many times he saw the Pope, Jimmy
Savile was always going to Hell.

When people ask me if I have a faith, a religion, I say yes.
My religion is Hypocrisy.

CLARE. I can't understand people who want to be on social
media all the time. It's so… shallow. There's nothing social
about it. Like. We had a work lunch the other day. Every
single person was on the phone. No one was talking. Two of
them were having a conversation on Facebook whilst they
were sitting next to each other. Next to each other! And one
of them wrote 'LOL' to a post. They wrote 'LOL' and they
didn't even actually laugh out loud.

I'm on it because… You have to be on social media. How
else are you going to talk to people?

I work in HR. Human resources. Who works where, for how
much, how to make the staff more efficient, more productive.
Resolve issues. That wasn't ever the dream. HR. The dream
was being an Olympic show-jumping champion. But I couldn't
ride, I had no horse. So, I read pony books. I read a lot when
I was younger. At night I'd read till after midnight. Every
night. Under the cover reading.

Only… It wasn't just because of the books, or cos I loved
ponies, it was… It was… Umm.

Beat.

Steve. Steve's my boyfriend. He's. He's great. We're great.
We're really great. He's not 'the one'. But he's… He's okay.
And we live together. Which is. Great.

Because.

The reason I read so much when I was younger. Until
I couldn't keep my eyes open... Was because... Because
I grew up in a haunted house.

Every night I slept there from the age of nine to seventeen,
there was a ghost in my bedroom.

JOSIE *at work. Reading a book at the front desk at Fix-U-
Fast Autos. A framed newspaper article on the wall with
a photo of* JOSIE *and her son,* MANNY. *Not prominent.*

JOSIE. I work at a garage in Lewisham. Front desk. It's quiet,
I don't have to engage with too many people. Got two
mechanics. They're alright. Y'know...

We don't bother each other. Which is good because the basic
chat here is – one of them talks shit, another one talks shit,
I point it out. End of conversation.

Same with the customers. Today, this woman came in.
Posh sort.

GRAHAM. I've been driving a black cab since I was twenty-nine.
I'll tell you my favourite passenger. An Arab.

I love the Arabs. It's like panning gold. They love a black cab
cos it's traditional. Once they get in, the meter could be
running all day. One fella I had, had lunch at The Savoy, had
me outside the whole time with the meter running. Even had
some food sent out for me. It was lovely. Tiny portion,
virtually nothing there but lovely. And I'd brought my
sandwiches. Cheese and onion. The fare was four hundred
quid and he gave me a tip. Two hundred and fifty quid! You
gotta love an Arab.

Met my wife in the cab. She was sat in the back with her
mate. Right chatterer. Came straight out and asked me for
my number. Liked what I was playing on the radio, liked my
aftershave, liked me. Asked me to pick her up the next day.

So, you know. I picked her up.

I don't make a habit of picking up women. Unless they're paying. Obviously.

Picked one up earlier. Near Fortnum and Mason. Heading for a garage in Lewisham. You know the kind. Posh. All in cream. Doesn't do her own washing. I asked if she was having a nice day. She said 'Hmm.'

I watched her in the mirror. Her eyes glued to her phone, like it was bluetoothing her lungs, like she couldn't breathe without it. She looked up. Asked why I wasn't turning left. So, I told her – said the road's closed. Cyclist's been hit.

Know what she said? 'Oh, shame, that way's much quicker.'

That's what road casualties are now to people like her – an inconvenience. When did that stop happening? Compassion?

JOSIE. She was all in cream. Looking at her phone, not me. I was busy. Doing my Sudoku. After a while, she realised she had to talk. Said I'd called. Said her car was ready. I asked for her name. On account of how I'm not psychic. I knew it before she even said it. There could only be one Hannah Greene-Brady. Greene with an 'e' on the end.

She told me she needed to get the car today, she had to pick up her daughter from university, so if I could…

Now, right. This is my favourite kind of person. Thinks they're all that. Well, if they're gonna play top trumps they better know who they're playing with.

I smiled. A rare occurrence. I said my son's at university.

She smiled back. Patronising like. Oh really, well my daughter's at Cambridge.

Oh yeah? I said. Which college? One of the old ones or one of the new ones?

Should've seen her face. Couldn't work out how I even knew to ask that question.

Emma's a first-year, Murray Edwards.

Oh. One of the new colleges. My son Manny's at Trinity.
Second year. It's one of the oldest. Looks like Hogwarts.

Cash or card?

MANNY. My mum always said it was a level playing field to
    get into Cambridge. Just work hard, Manny. Get your grades.
    So, I did, I worked really fucking hard. And I got the grades.
    Two A-stars and an A. Everyone told me I deserved to be
    there. Mum, Granddad, my boys. Everyone was made up.
    The local paper even wrote about it.

    But Mum and me spent so long thinking about the
    destination, we didn't think about what it would be like to
    actually be there. It ain't easy. It ain't easy being me there.

    On my first week, one of the other students asked if I'd got
    there on disadvantage points. That's a thing now – the
    disadvantage points. Being in care is one of them, having
    a state education is another. The actual fact of having a state
    education is seen as a disadvantage. Read that in the
    university newspaper. I mean… [WTF?]

    I thought I'd meet other people like me. Normal. But I didn't
    find any for weeks. It was like they were in hiding. I was
    surrounded by people from private school. They *all* knew
    each other. They weren't doing this alone.

    I'd always thought Cambridge was saved for the most special,
    the ones who work the hardest. Who study. The brightest. But
    it's not a level playing field. Those students knew they were
    special from the moment their parents started paying for their
    education. It's drilled into them at school, to have that
    confidence to think that what they say matters, that they can
    do it, they deserve it, fuck everyone else!

    Only have to look at the Government to see that, right?

    My first week, I went up to a group. Hadn't realised they all
    knew each other from school and ski trips. I thought they'd
    be feeling like me – out of their depth, looking for mates.
    I went up to them, asked if I could join them? Know the first

thing they said? They said they were 'full'. Their friendship group was full.

I just thought – fuck you.

Sorry, no. I tell a lie. That wasn't the first thing they said to me. The first thing they said was could I clear their plates?

CLARE. Steve! Guess who I had in my office today? Clive. Clive from accounts? Clive who wears a cardigan even when it's thirty degrees out? He'd hugged Sonya from marketing on her way out of the tearoom. No one else around. Little quiet corner and he hugged her.

I said to him – Clive, you must see that wasn't an appropriate way to behave. He said he was being nice; it was Sonya's birthday. He liked to give hugs on birthdays. Not here, not at work, I told him. She didn't ask for you to hug her. She'd specifically asked you before not to hug her. And she's not the first.

Five women have said he's hugged them. Same spot too. Clive said he was just being warm. Friendly. He's just a pervert. Course I couldn't say that. Instead, I said people have boundaries, Clive. You have to respect that. If it was just being friendly, why do it in places where you won't be seen by anyone else?

Half an hour later I've got Zara in my office. She'd been crying over the photocopier. Literally just stood there crying. I brought her in. Got the Kleenex out.

She said she wasn't sleeping. She couldn't stop worrying. She worried all the time. Was worried her son would stop breathing. That's why she couldn't sleep. Had to keep checking on him. I asked if her son was sick? He wasn't. There was nothing wrong with him. Zara had barely slept in months.

I suggested she might need some time off. Get some help. I said she was brave. I said asking for help is a sign of strength, not weakness.

I ask for help all the time, I told her. All the time.

I can't stop asking for help.

I just don't ever ask for it out loud.

She looks sharply offstage. Scared. And back.

Woodside Hospice. ANGE *at work.*

ANGE. People are always surprised when they come to our hospice. They think it'll look like a hospital. We're more like a five-star hotel. Blonde, beautiful, comfortable, clean. Big windows, lots of light. It's got to be lovely. It's a hospice. We've had more than a dozen extensions. It always has to get bigger. People are always dying.

Death never stops.

We have in-patients who are reaching the end of their lives. We don't have visiting restrictions, you can have flowers, your loved ones can stay.

And we also have out-patients five days a week. We're meant to have ten patients a day but it's always around fourteen. Even death has to be financially viable. We have one aim – to give the best symptom control possible. Medical treatment, occupational and holistic therapy. We have to be holistic. It's not just about our patients' physical pain. It's about where they're at in their heads. How they're feeling. It's all linked.

We work a lot with their families. It's important patients have loving and supportive relationships with those around them. Important the family doesn't fall to bits. That they're close.

Her phone buzzes with a text, she reads it.

Sorry. It's my sister. She's a fucking pain in the arse. She… It doesn't matter.

I've started making a memory box with Elsie, one of our out-patients. Elsie's very anxious. Picks at her neck when she's worried. Makes it sore. I thought a memory box would take her mind off it. Only she started getting anxious about what kind of memory it had to be. Started picking her neck even more. I suggested maybe one with her sister – cos her sister had brought her in.

Elsie's face lit up, she said about when her and her sister went to look at the Christmas lights on Piccadilly. They were only young. Teenagers. They were outside a hotel when this man in a trilby walked out. Elsie recognised him straight away. Frank Sinatra. She couldn't stop herself; she ran straight over. She said he was a gentleman. He let her put on his hat. And his eyes, she said, they really were blue. He kissed Elsie's cheeks. Said 'Don't tell my wife!'

I said as memories go, Elsie. I think that sounds like a bloody good one.

It was like she was a teenager again. She couldn't wait to see her sister and remind her about it. Put on some Frank Sinatra when they got home.

I can't remember the last time I actually wanted to see my sister.

The Butcher's Slab. CLARE *drinks alone. Bottle of wine. Two glasses. Her bag.*

CLARE. A wanker.

A wanker. That's what Steve my boyfriend's just called me in front of everyone. The people from my office over there are pretending they didn't hear when they very obviously did. All I said was I'd booked the indoor skydiving. He said he'd wanted to try it when I told him about it, so I'd booked it for this weekend.

He started complaining, saying I made him do things every weekend. Which isn't correct. I said it'll be fun, he'd love it. That it's good to try new things. Work hard. Play hard.

And that was when he said it.

D'you know who says 'work hard, play hard'? A wanker.

Her phone rings. She cuts it off.

I'm not going to answer. He can just think about what he's said.

GRAHAM *enters, driving mode.*

GRAHAM. I've got into talk radio. I like the phone-ins. Makes you feel part of it.

I can't stand silence. Hate it. Cos then… Cos then.

Well. Silence is the worst.

Flashback: The sound of a young child and baby playing. BEX emerges, shuts a door. The sound of the children now muffled. Something inside her threatening to erupt. She can't contain herself any more.

She screams. Silently. Screams and screams and screams. The silence makes it all the more violent.

JOSIE's flat. The table laid. An old hi-fi on the side. The plant pot in the corner. A framed newspaper article about MANNY on the wall. The same one as in the garage.

JOSIE *paces, makes a call.*

JOSIE. I don't know if your phone's run out of battery or if you're on the Tube but… Let me know when you're going to be back. You said you'd be here an hour ago.

She hangs up. A faint panting is heard. JOSIE paces.

Keys in the door. MANNY enters. Carries a rucksack and a suitcase on wheels. His whole life. JOSIE hugs him, unbalances him.

MANNY. Hold on.

He pulls away. Throughout the following, MANNY tries to defuse every situation, to stop his mother from going off. He's a ninja at keeping calm. It's fucking tough.

Sorry. I… Let me get this off.

That's better.

JOSIE *hugs him quickly then immediately pushes him away from her.*

JOSIE. Let me look at you. You've lost weight. Are you eating?

MANNY. Course I am.

JOSIE *eyeballs him.*

JOSIE. Surprised you told me you were actually coming back. I've been calling you for weeks. Texting but you don't reply.

MANNY. Yeah, sorry. It's been busy. Been studying, in the library. Not allowed phones. I replied to some of them.

JOSIE. Seven. In ten weeks.

MANNY. I'm sorry, alright, I'm sorry. I'm sorry.

Beat.

It's weird. Queenie not being here. She'd have been all over me. Wanting a cuddle. First Granddad goes, then Queenie.

JOSIE. Yeah, well I'll be next.

MANNY. That's cheery. Thanks for that, Mum.

Takes in the hi-fi.

Got Granddad's hi-fi working?

JOSIE. Nah. Lead's bust. Like the look of it. It's furniture. Useful. I can put my coffee on it.

MANNY. And it's like having a bit of Granddad in the room. Must be. Must be missing him.

JOSIE doesn't answer and MANNY doesn't notice. He takes in the plant.

That where Queenie is?

JOSIE. So you read that text then?

MANNY ignores her.

MANNY. It's quiet without her.

JOSIE. Yeah.

She changes the conversation, gets the meal ready. MANNY tries to speak throughout the following, but he doesn't get a chance.

I made your favourite for tea. Brown-stew chicken and dumplings. Are you enjoying those formal dinners? I saw some photos online, on the college's Facebook page. You're allowed to take guests. I could come to one.

MANNY (*interrupts*). Mum, no. No. You wouldn't like it. We have to wear gowns and, you know you think all that stuff's elitist bollocks.

JOSIE. Yeah, but not when you do it. When you do it, it's something to be proud of. It's an achievement. It's brilliant! I'm not gonna embarrass you, if that's what you're worried about.

MANNY. No, course not. I… I don't know. Next term's busy with exams. Maybe term after.

JOSIE. Alright. So. Tell me. What did your supervisor say?

MANNY. She said I'm looking at a First.

JOSIE. A First?

MANNY. Possibly. A low First.

JOSIE. A bloody First. We did it! I knew we could do it!

MANNY. It's only a low First. And it's predicted, I haven't got it.

JOSIE. Yeah, but it's a First. From Cambridge. That'll teach them. You're showing them. All of them. A First!

MANNY. Who are you talking about? Showing who?

JOSIE. Them. People. Everyone. Your old headteacher! He still
comes into the garage to service his crappy little Peugeot.
I might tell him. No. I will tell him. And after he excluded
you too. Bet he'll feel stupid when I tell him.

MANNY. No. Don't. He's not worth your energy. I'm just glad
I left. I hated that school.

JOSIE. It wasn't the school you hated; it was him. Because he
never gave you a chance. Never recognised your potential.
Lewisham College have still got that newspaper article on
display.

MANNY looks at the newspaper article she's got displayed.

What about your friends at university? How's your house?
Still mates with Jacob? Anyone else in the African Caribbean
Society or is it still just you and the cleaner?

MANNY (*serious*). That's actually racist, Mum.

JOSIE. Fuck off.

I was thinking. You should ask some of your university
friends over here. Bet they'd love to have a place to stay in
London.

MANNY. Mum, half of Cambridge live in London. People'll
have bigger places to stay.

JOSIE. Oh, right. So, you don't want anyone to stay, is that it?
Don't be ashamed of where you're from, Manny.

MANNY. I'm not, I… That wasn't what I meant. I literally
meant they'll have bigger places to stay. Places with spare
rooms. Y'know – beds. But maybe, yeah. Maybe.

JOSIE. Oh. Yeah. Okay.

Beat.

MANNY. I still can't get my head round it. Granddad not being
here. He'd have been so happy about what my supervisor said.

JOSIE. Yeah.

Your education was more important to him than anything.

Beat.

Why aren't you posting on Instagram any more?

MANNY. Oh, no… You're not stalking me again? I'm going to have to block you.

JOSIE. It's not stalking. It's taking an interest! Don't you even think about blocking me. If you don't phone me, how else am I meant to find out what you're doing? Telepathy?

MANNY. Wait until you see me?

JOSIE. What? Ten weeks? Met a woman at work today whose daughter's at Cambridge. First year. She was about to go off and pick her up. You've never asked me to do that. Pick you up.

MANNY. Why would I…?

JOSIE. It could have been me there.

MANNY *grimaces, waits for it. Heard this a million times.*

That's what my teacher said.

MANNY. I know, you've [told me] –

JOSIE (*interrupts*). She said I had potential. She said Oxford but that's the same thing as Cambridge. But I never applied myself, not like you. You put your head down, worked. You didn't go out, you focused. Nothing else mattered.

That's why this is so important. You've got to keep your eye on the prize, Manny. A First from Cambridge? With a degree like that you can do anything, go anywhere. We have to stay focused.

You sit down. I'll get your supper.

Manny, sit down.

MANNY. Oh. I should've said. I said I'd meet Raoul. Some of the others. I got a burger at the station. I'll eat it later. Brown stew's always better the next day, you say.

He grabs his coat.

I'll sort my stuff out tomorrow. Don't wait up.

He gives her a quick kiss, she's unresponsive, hurt. Doesn't look at him as he leaves.

ANGE *in Suki's, a nightclub. Unsettled.*

ANGE. Have you noticed how when you ask someone if they're okay, they don't tell you?

Not how they really feel. They're too worried what you'll think of them, that you'll judge them, cos they're ashamed or whatever the fuck. People are never fucking honest.

What I love most about my job is the communication. People who are poorly, really poorly know they don't have long. They're not arsed about being polite. When you ask them, they tell you. They're not worried they're being indiscreet. They don't have time for that. Every second counts.

Why do we do that? Why do we hide how we feel?

The way I see it, I think if you're worrying about the things you don't have to worry about, then you don't have time to worry about the things you should be worrying about.

Me and my sister. We're never honest. Never. She doesn't even like me. Everything's a criticism even her praise. She always sees the negative in everything. The risks. She says she's just being practical but I…

And we just can't. We don't.

We don't [connect]…

Oh my God, we were close, growing up. She was three years older. I looked up to her so much, my bigger sister. Worshipped her. We got up to all sorts. Bloody nightmare. Mum wanted four children. After us, she made Dad get the snip.

We did everything together. Me and my sister.

Everything.

We were so close; we could feel what the other was feeling. That bond? That…?

And then. It stopped. Eight years ago. We broke.

And it…

I thank fuck neither of us is dying.

Because then we might actually have to deal with each other.

ANGE *dances, concentrates. Wants to forget her sister. Just wants to come up… up.*

CLARE*'s flat. She looks lonely. Small. Alone.*

CLARE. Turns out Steve hadn't been calling me to say he was sorry. He'd been calling me to say.

To say it was over. His bags were packed, he was waiting for me so he could explain.

I presumed he'd met someone else. That's what men normally do, isn't it? Get a newer model. But no, no. It was me. Because of me. I asked if it was because of the indoor skydiving. He said it wasn't.

Apparently, life's too short to be with second best, someone who's not 'the one'.

I said, how dare you say I'm second best and he said no, he was. He was talking about me.

He wanted me to be honest with myself. Admit I didn't want to be with him. He didn't think I ever had. Didn't think I even liked him.

He said I couldn't have sex unless I was pissed.

He said there's something wrong with me.

Beat.

He accused me of not wanting to be on my own. Asked if that was why I wanted him to move in the night we met.

I said no, that was stupid. I said I like you, Steve, I fancy you.

That was when he asked if I loved him and I...

The sound of a door banging shut.

So, now I'm alone. But I don't think I am.

I don't think it's places that are haunted. I think it's people.

CLARE *looks offstage, scared. Drags her eyes back.*

And I. I think it's back.

I think it's been waiting for me to be by myself.

The beginning of a shadow creeps into her space.

GRAHAM *at work, driving his cab.*

GRAHAM. I'm having trouble concentrating.

I find myself starting down a road and forgetting to turn off.

I drive miles. Just keep driving straight ahead. I ended up in Dorking yesterday. Took me over two hours to drive back. I hate the A3212.

I get lost.

Terrible thing for a taxi driver to admit.

It's just. It feels like there's been too much change. Sounds are different. Shapes are blurred. The whole world's changed colour.

Flashback: BEX *in the back of his cab. She wears a wig; she plays with it throughout. This is a game they play – strangers in a cab like the first time they met. We should believe they're strangers throughout.*

BEX. Hey mate, I heard your cab's free if it's to a hospice.

GRAHAM. Nah, that's only kids going to Great Ormond Street Hospital. There are only two things you get free cab rides for – those kiddies and a cabby's first passenger.

BEX. Oh right. So having cancer doesn't count? Gotta get something for free if I've gotta wear this wig. Itches like fuck.

GRAHAM. Go on then. You can ride for free. I don't say that to everyone, mind.

BEX. Should hope not. You'll end up broke. Your missus wouldn't like that.

GRAHAM. She'd kill me. She always says I'm too soft-hearted. Says I spoil the kids. I think I spoil her.

BEX. My husband's a bit of a twat.

GRAHAM. Bit harsh.

BEX. Mind has a habit of wandering. Found a BabyGro in the dishwasher today.

GRAHAM. That's having little 'uns. It gives you nappy brain.

BEX. He's not bad for a twat, I s'pose.

They're at the hospice.

Is this it?

She leaves GRAHAM, *who's left alone.*

Present day. GRAHAM *keeps driving. It should all feel like the present.*

GRAHAM. Had to pick my eldest up in the middle of the night last week. He's only little. Four. Was staying with cousins in Bedfordshire. It's flat, Bedfordshire. Nothing but sky. You can see the stars. Less light pollution. In London the night's not black, it's orange. So, my boy was lying under a skylight, looking up at the stars when his cousin turns to him and says –

Have you seen *The Lion King*? Do you know what stars are? They're dead people.

He told him his nana and granddad were up there. Along with everyone else.

That was it. All my boy could see was a sky full of dead people. Staring at him. Bloody *Lion King*. Well… I had to get him. Made me glad we have orange skies.

Beat.

My wife left me three months ago.

Flashback: Woodside Hospice, BEX enters. She looks anxious. Her wig is now on straight. ANGE enters.

ANGE. Can I help you?

BEX. I got a letter, saying to come. My name's Rebecca Williams – Bex.

Hands the letter over.

ANGE. Thanks. I'm Ange.

BEX. Feeling a bit nervous to be honest. Coming here.

I really want a cigarette. Is that a bad thing to say when you've got cancer?

ANGE. We've got a smoking shelter in the garden, if you like I can take you?

BEX. Oh, I don't smoke. I gave up years ago. Before I got pregnant with my first. Just this. Coming here.

ANGE. Well, it's normal to be nervous.

BEX. Yeah.

I didn't catch your name. I'm really shit with names. I've forgotten yours, sorry.

ANGE. It's okay. Ange.

BEX. My mum's name. I won't forget that.

It looks better than I thought. Thought it'd be. Depressing. Bit… Morbid. It's alright though. Peaceful. Nice. What are they doing?

ANGE. Tai chi.

BEX. Oh right. On chairs. Never seen people do it on chairs before. I do tai chi too. Not on a chair. And yoga.

ANGE. We do yoga here.

BEX. I'm not going to be here long. At the hospice, I mean. I'm only here to keep my fella happy. Wouldn't shut up about it. I said it was giving up, coming here. He said maybe it could help, but...

I know they said it's terminal but they're not always right, are they? I'm going to get better. There's always a way out. There's always hope.

ANGE. Hope is very important.

They both sit. ANGE *opens a file.*

BEX. I'd just had Luke, my second son. He's one now, Bradley's three. Thought it was a blocked milk duct. Mastitis. That's what my doctor thought. I thought I just needed some antibiotics. I didn't know... I mean, I'd just had a baby.

It's not going to kill me. It's not. People recover from breast cancer all the time. Me and my fella did a lot of research. Reading up about it. He said he'd never spent so much time googling tits. Yeah, well that's not true.

She and ANGE *giggle.*

It spread to my liver.

I'll get better. I like positivity. Visualisation. Seeing myself well and healthy. Visualising the cancer shrinking. I meditate. I swim. I don't drink alcohol any more which is a total pain in the arse cos I could murder a glass of wine half the time.

ANGE. Yeah, me too.

BEX. I eat clean food. Vegan. Nothing processed. Everything cooked from scratch. No chemicals.

Apart from the chemo. Obviously. But it's working... It is working.

Looks round.

So how does this work then?

ANGE. Well, let's start by you telling me what a good day would look like for you?

BEX. Starts with getting enough sleep. But... I find nights hard. Can I say this? Should I just concentrate on the positives?

ANGE. You can say whatever you want to me. However you want to say it.

Beat.

BEX. Well my fella, he works nights. We thought it would be for the best. He's around to look after the kids in the day. Has some sleep whilst they're at nursery. Goes to work, once they're in bed. Only, at night, when you're on your own, when no one else is awake, it's...

God, I haven't told anyone this. Wanted to keep positive, but it's lonely. And I can cope with anything, so long as I don't feel like I'm alone.

ANGE. Course. That's normal.

BEX. Sometimes I distract myself. Send my husband photos of my wig whilst he's working. I put things in it, put it on things. Stupid things. Make him laugh. Make me laugh. He said we should give the wig its own Instagram page.

I was with my consultant last week and every time he looked away; I turned my wig back-to-front. See if he'd say anything. See if I could make him laugh.

ANGE. Did he?

BEX. Nah, it was Mr Barrington. I farted in front of him once, when I was bending down to pick my bag up. Didn't crack a smile. That's sad, innit? When you can't laugh at a fart.

I find it hard to sleep. It's not the cancer. Well not just that.
Sometimes I don't get to sleep till four or five in the
morning. Then Bradley comes in, wakes me at the crack of
dawn. Little cunt.

I don't mean that. Obviously I don't really think he's a cunt.

ANGE *bursts out laughing*. BEX *smiles*. *She catches sight of*
ANGE*'s wrist – a star tattoo*.

Look! Oh my God. We've got the same star tattoo. Snap.
Fucking hell!

She reveals the same tattoo.

That's the universe that is. That's a sign.

JOSIE *in her quiet place – a promontory on the Thames,*
near the Oxo Tower Wharf on the South Bank. She stands
alone at the end. GRAHAM *on his own, too.*

JOSIE. I used to come here with Queenie. I loved this place,
ever since I was a little girl. Dad. My dad told me if you
stand right at the end of the promontory and focus on
something floating on top like – a duck, say, or a seagull.
It's like *you're* sailing and *they're* the ones keeping still.
Like you're floating up the Thames.

GRAHAM. Between 4 and 5 a.m., it's dead. I like driving then.
Like the solitude. There's the odd fare, not many. The only
ones around are the homeless and the street cleaners. The
stray drunk.

Just been across Westminster Bridge. The only vehicle.

JOSIE. And it's quiet. Not as many tourists. Can't move for
tourists on the South Bank. None of them know how to walk
on a bloody pavement. Three, four, five in a row. Great big
rucksacks on, knocking you over whenever they turn.

GRAHAM. I don't want to go home.

JOSIE. Someone should make an app for that. How to walk on
pavements.

What do you think, Queenie?

She looks down to her left.

I keep forgetting. You're not there.

She looks back down again then up. Looks totally alone.

CLARE*'s flat. It's dark. Dimly lit. Ghost-story time.* CLARE *puts on some music. Can't stand silence. She's tense, watching shadows. Throughout this speech we should get a sense the darkness is encroaching on her. Of something hiding in the shadows.*

CLARE. I was nine when my parents moved there, to the house. It was big. Detached.

Not old, maybe only fifty years. Five bedrooms. Two at the front, a long corridor, then three bedrooms at the back.

Soon after we moved in, my little sister wanted to swap bedrooms. She had one at the front. Said she couldn't sleep there. So, we swapped.

She never said why she couldn't sleep there.

Month or so later, I woke up. It was dark. The room was pitch black. But there… At the bottom of my bed, I saw… I saw a figure. Like a. Like a white dress coming together. Only told Auntie Maggie. She seemed like the obvious person to tell. She used to tell us ghost stories when we used to stay over at hers, then drag us to church the next morning. She and Uncle Billy didn't have kids.

She said it must have been car lights reflecting off my mirror. But the thing is, I know my curtains were closed. I know it was pitch black.

I didn't tell her what happened next. I haven't told anyone.

CLARE *looks towards her bedroom. A creak from the wardrobe. Quiet. She drags her eyes back to the front.*

Week later, I woke up again in the middle of the night. Thought I'd heard a noise. I don't know what. My heart was pounding. I couldn't see anything.

But I heard something.

From the other side of the room, I could hear the sound of breathing. There was another presence in my room. I thought maybe it was me I could hear. I held my breath, but I could still hear breathing.

And I… I heard it every night I slept in that room.

She drinks wine.

I've felt something here. Since Steve left.

She turns her music up.

I'm finding it hard to sleep again.

She drinks wine.

Because that's when it comes. When I'm alone in my bedroom.

She drinks wine. A creak as her wardrobe door opens slowly.

JOSIE*'s. She enters, in her dressing gown.* MANNY, *bright, he's been waiting for her.*

MANNY. Happy birthday.

JOSIE. I'm forty-nine, what's to be happy about? Didn't think you'd be here. Thought you'd been avoiding me.

MANNY. I needed to earn money.

JOSIE. I don't want you tiring yourself before you go back. I can do more hours.

MANNY. I'm a grown man. I can support myself. I should.

Takes out money.

That's to cover my rent and bills.

JOSIE. No. Don't. I don't want it. Keep it for college.

MANNY. Mum, take it. Get something new. Treat yourself.

JOSIE. Thank you.

MANNY. You're welcome.

   What?

JOSIE. I got you a present. Was going to give it to you the night
   you arrived but you...

MANNY. Nah, no, no. That's not how it works, Mum. Not on
   your birthday.

   He hands her a wrapped-up box – shoebox size.

JOSIE. Not shoes? You know I don't like anyone buying me
   shoes. The size is never right. I've got broad feet.

MANNY. I'm well aware of that fact. It's not shoes. Open it.

   JOSIE *pulls out a handful of dirty-looking tapes.*

JOSIE. Tapes? I haven't even got a tape player.

MANNY. Get a new lead for the hi-fi. Look on eBay.

   It's me and Granddad talking. It was for a school project. I'd
   forgotten about it – found them when we were cleaning out
   his house and. And I thought it would be nice to listen. Now,
   he's gone. Be like you've still got a bit of him.

JOSIE. Your granddad made a lot of sense, did he, after six
   pints of Guinness?

MANNY. I did them all at the start of the day. After breakfast.
   Before The Red Lion.

JOSIE. Or The Crown or The Black Dog. Well done. Quite
   a feat.

MANNY. He said I should write a book about him. Said it'd
   make us rich.

JOSIE. For his stories? Be lucky if you get twenty pee.

MANNY. I think you should listen to them.

We've hardly talked about him, Granddad. You've said more about Queenie than him.

JOSIE. You've not been here. Well, this has really cheered me up on my birthday.

Pushes tapes away.

I don't want them. I heard enough from him when he was alive. I don't need to go through that again. Bring it all up. I don't want it.

MANNY. They're not like that. Mum, it's not what you think. I wouldn't give you something that I thought would upset you. They're nice. Look. Think about it later, maybe.

I got you this too.

He hands over an envelope. JOSIE *pulls out a voucher.*

JOSIE. An adult-education voucher?

MANNY. It's for Lewisham College. You can use it for any course.

It's like you said, could have been you at university. It's never too late.

JOSIE. I don't have time for classes. I've got work. I don't want to be with a load of dropouts and weirdos. There's always someone strange you don't want to sit next to –

MANNY. Probably you in this case.

I just thought you could do something you're interested in. Whatever. It'll be something different to do.

JOSIE*'s not listening, she's fetching* MANNY*'s present.*

JOSIE. This is what I got you. Go on, open it.

MANNY *opens it, it's a brand-new gown for Trinity, his college at Cambridge.*

Go on then. Put it on.

MANNY. I've got a gown, already.

JOSIE. Yeah, but it's second hand. The stitching's all coming undone. This is proper. Go on, put it on.

Reluctantly, MANNY *puts it on.*

Ooh, let me get my phone. Hold on.

She heads offstage. MANNY *takes off the gown, puts it down.*

He feels like he can't breathe. He exits.

JOSIE *returns, finds the room empty.*

Time passes. Domestic glimpses.

CLARE *gets ready for work, hungover.*

JOSIE *and* MANNY *keep missing each other. As one enters a room, the other exits.*

BEX *tries to walk across a room, but a child keeps attaching themselves to a leg.*

ANGE *finishes doing yoga, starts rolling a spliff.*

GRAHAM *haunted. Unable to move. It takes a gargantuan effort to even stand.*

Woodside Hospice. ANGE *in super-efficient mode deals with everything. Patients, meetings, a tai chi class. Memory boxes…*

ANGE. Death. It never stops. Every death takes a little bit from you.

Suki's. The lights come back on, ANGE *in her club, downing shots.*

But being there when people die… It's a gift. A privilege. I learn things from each of my patients. I know, I know, it sounds cheesy. But it's true. I know what I get out of my job. It's not about money. If it was about that, I'd have left years ago.

I'm lucky to do my job. How many other jobs can you say that about?

Still not seen my sister. She's too busy. Not talked in… I don't know.

She's stopped texting. We live in the same city, we're on the same Tube line. You have to put more effort into avoiding each other than you'd think.

The Butcher's Slab, CLARE *is drunk, a hot mess. Keeps dropping her phone.*

CLARE. They're looking at me. The people from the office. They think I can't see them. But I can. (*Squints.*) Over there!

I've been looking busy on my phone.

Squints at phone. Laughs abruptly.

Pretend funny text.

She looks sharply over at invisible co-workers and glowers. Calls over.

What? What are you looking at? Seen something funny? Never seen a woman having a good time on her own before, Clive?

Well fuck you. Fuck the lot of you.

CLARE *outside. She can barely stand. She puts an arm out.*

Taxi!

GRAHAM *pulls up. Eyes her suspiciously.*

Muswell Hill.

CLARE *gets in.* GRAHAM *eyes her, worried she'll hurl.* CLARE *does her best to appear sober.*

They travel in silence. Billy Fury's 'I Will' plays low on the radio. CLARE doesn't notice it. GRAHAM turns the radio up.

Turn it off.

GRAHAM. Y'what, love?

CLARE. Will you turn the radio off?

Please.

GRAHAM turns it off. Silence.

They get out of the cab. CLARE nearly falls over. GRAHAM gives her his arm.

CLARE and GRAHAM enter a small lift. Travel up. CLARE pissed, trying not to show it. GRAHAM trying to act oblivious.

As the lift opens, CLARE heads towards her door, supported by GRAHAM. At her front door, he leaves her. CLARE, upset to be left alone. She calls out as the lift doors close on GRAHAM.

I'm being haunted.

GRAHAM disappears. CLARE doesn't want to enter her flat. She has to force herself.

CLARE's flat. It should feel like a flat from a horror film. All shadows and atmosphere. CLARE, terrified, walks straight to her bed. Climbs in. Performs her decades-long ritual – tucking the covers under her body. Putting out a crucifix. A lavender bag.

A noise, a creak. CLARE sits up – a neighbour upstairs or…? She turns her radio on, low.

The breathing starts to get louder. Underneath it, a distorted Billy Fury's 'I Will' plays.

Fix-U-Fast Autos. JOSIE *on the front desk, pauses from scrolling through her phone.*

JOSIE. Manny wouldn't say why he left.

Beat.

I've been checking his emails. I was worried. Anyway, his supervisor's happy with him. Should see his reading list, the number of books he's got to get through. No wonder I never see him.

Beat.

I just read on here that if you hug someone for twenty seconds, your body creates pheromones. Feel-good vibes.

If anyone tried to hug me for twenty seconds I'd punch their fucking lights out.

A London park. CLARE *exercises outside.*

CLARE. I've had to give up alcohol.

I can't remember how I got home the other night. It's a blur. My sister texted the next day. Apparently, I called her six times. I don't remember.

I've got into exercise.

I'm treating it like a project.

Time jumps forward.

I've been dry thirty days. I've got a Fitbit. I'm getting toned. I'm also on Night Nurse.

It's great. It's working. It really is working. Well… Apart from the palpitations and the runs and the upset tummy, but that's just because of the Night Nurse!

It's all good!

Time jumps forward again. CLARE *still exercising, but tired now.*

Been dry sixty days. I had to give up the Night Nurse. Had to talk to my GP – I had to be careful about what I said. Don't want them to think I'm 'mad'.

She looks mad.

I'm not mad. I'm just... focused.

My GP asked if I could be stressed? I said of course I'm stressed I'm not sleeping. I just want sleeping tablets. They said that wasn't the answer. Said maybe I should talk to someone?

They were fuck-all help. Fuck 'em.

I've got sleeping tablets. Over-the-counter. I have to be careful. Go to different chemists, so they don't realise it's all for me. Pharmacists can be so nosy.

But it's all good!

Her phone rings. CLARE *freezes.*

Flashback: ANGE *at the hospice, she joins* BEX *who's there as a visitor. She looks well. Her hair now short and curly, no wig.*

BEX. I'm in remission. Told you I'd beat it.

ANGE. I heard.

ANGE *hugs* BEX *tight. Emotional.*

BEX. I wanted to tell you in person. Y'know cos, you know. The universe.

ANGE. I'm so pleased for you.

BEX. Yeah, well I said, didn't I? Being positive.

I want to do something for the hospice. A fundraiser. Buy more drinks for the drinks trolley. The volunteers are always nicking the vodka.

ANGE. Which ones?

BEX. The Christians. They're a bloody nightmare. I heard one saying that she wouldn't tidy a cupboard cos that wasn't why Jesus sent her here, to do the work of a cleaner.

I said – Jesus washed the feet of lepers, love. One–nil against the Christians. So, I'm doing a fundraiser. Say thank you.

ANGE. Thank you.

BEX. I should let you go, you'll be busy.

ANGE. Yeah.

BEX. Yeah. I should go. Only.

My fella's scared, Ange, and I don't know what to do. He thinks he's in one of those horror films where you think the monster's dead, but it comes back to get you in the last few minutes. It's pissing me off. It's all done now.

ANGE. Give it time. Be gentle. Be as kind to him as you would to a stranger. We're always nicer to strangers than our families.

BEX. Yeah. How's your sister?

ANGE. What?

BEX. Your sister? You mentioned her last time.

ANGE. Bex, we're not here to talk about me.

BEX. Why not? You've heard me going on for months. Have you spoken to her yet?

ANGE. I've texted.

BEX. And?

ANGE. And she's not replied.

BEX. So, call her. Go and see her.

ANGE. No, thanks. Look, it really doesn't matter.

BEX. Course it matters. What's going on?

ANGE. What is this, twenty questions?

We're just not close that's all. Not been close for years. It's fine.

BEX. Is it? Sounds a bit shit to me. Go and see her. That's what you'd tell us to do.

ANGE. That wouldn't work. I can't talk to her. Bex, can we talk about you?

BEX. You're being a hypocrite.

ANGE (*laughs*). That's my religion.

BEX. Is that meant to be funny?

ANGE. It was only a joke.

Beat.

BEX. No, it's not. You say it all the time. It's not something to be proud of, being a hypocrite. You don't get a pass just because you work with people who are dying. Sort your house out, Ange.

BEX walks off.

Present day. ANGE busy with a task. GRAHAM enters. Uncomfortable.

GRAHAM. Jennifer Walsh? Meant to be picking her up.

ANGE. I'll find her, why don't you come in and wait?

ANGE walks towards him, but he backs away.

GRAHAM. No, no you're alright. I'll be outside.

He walks away.

ANGE. Talking's overrated. Sometimes I just want to. I want to… Escape. Be happy.

She suddenly plunged into Suki's. Takes a pill.

Can't give a fuck, if you're fucked, right?

The music pulls her up.

As she dances, she sees MANNY. He sees her. A smile shared. She circles him, he circles her. Flirting without words. They move closer until they're stroking, kissing…

They tumble into ANGE*'s flat.* ANGE *pulls off her top layer of clothes.*

It's hot. Are you hot? The club was boiling.

MANNY. My ears are ringing.

ANGE. I'm thirsty. I need a drink. Want a drink, Manny?

She heads off to get tequila. MANNY *takes in the flat.*

Make yourself more comfortable.

MANNY *awkward. Did she mean...? Should he...? He quickly pulls off his shirt and jeans. Checks he doesn't smell.*

MANNY. I got myself more comfortable.

ANGE *enters with two glasses and tequila. Now wearing T-shirt and trousers.* MANNY *embarrassed. Quickly grabs his clothes and puts them back on.*

Shit. I thought you meant. When you said get comfortable. I thought you meant.

ANGE. It's fine. It doesn't matter. It's okay.

She pours two tequilas, hands one over. Downs hers. MANNY *sips his.*

MANNY. Nice place you've got here. It's...

ANGE *pours more tequila, starts skinning up.*

ANGE. It's cheap. A co-op. Everyone here works in essential services. Got fire officers, a paramedic, couple of nurses. We're great in an emergency!

MANNY. Okay... You're not police, are you?

ANGE. God, no. No. I'm a... a... An international spy.

MANNY. Oh right... Right. I'm... I'm a global peacekeeper.

ANGE. Nice.

ANGE *begins to unbutton* MANNY*'s shirt.*

MANNY. You ever go undercover?

ANGE. I love going undercover.

She takes off his shirt.

How's peacekeeping?

He pushes ANGE back, pulls off her trousers.

MANNY. Hard.

He realises the innuendo, sniggers, ANGE sniggers too.

ANGE. How old are you? Actually, how old are you?

MANNY. Does it matter?

ANGE. No. I'm interested.

MANNY. I'm twenty-three.

ANGE. Oh my God, you're a baby. I'm thirty-four.

MANNY. Thirty-four? Wow. You look good. Don't look old at all.

ANGE. I'm not. Old.

They get close, about to kiss.

MANNY. Not old enough to be my mum, anyway.

ANGE pushes him away.

What? That was a joke. My mum's way older than you.

ANGE. I don't want you to think about your mum when we're…

MANNY. I'm not. Well, I am now, obviously. I shouldn't have said anything, I'm sorry.

ANGE. Family's the last fucking thing I want to think about.

She starts crying.

I don't know why I'm doing this. Why am I crying?

Beat.

It's fine, it's just the come-down. I've got some bombs. Do you want one?

MANNY. I don't think that's a good idea. I've got a double shift tomorrow.

ANGE. Global peacekeepers have to do double shifts?

Come on. It's an excellent idea. Instant happiness! Escape.

She tries to embrace him, but he moves back. Uncomfortable. Coming down fast.

MANNY. It's late. I feel a bit weird now.

ANGE. That's the come-down, that's all. You need to relax. Let me give you a massage. Sit down.

MANNY *likes the sound of that. He sits.* ANGE *starts massaging him, expertly.*

That feels better, doesn't it?

MANNY. That's good. Really good.

He gets into it.

ANGE. I don't know why I was crying.

That's not true, I do. I said family and I just got this image of my sister and.

She feels more tears coming, squashes them back down inside. Starts massaging harder.

We haven't talked in a long time.

Because… There's stuff we haven't talked about. Because there's stuff…

MANNY *winces, she's massaging too hard.*

We never see each other.

MANNY *winces again. This isn't the sexy massage he was hoping for. He twists round. Strokes* ANGE's *arm. Gentle.*

She's angry with me.

Let's forget it. Start again. No words. We don't need words.

They kiss. Start getting intimate. As MANNY's *hand slips down,* ANGE *pulls sharply away.*

When we were little, me and my sister used to stay at my Auntie Maggie's. Once a month. Till we were teenagers. Only. Only the thing was. You see. Auntie Maggie got a new boyfriend. Married after six months. Made us call him 'uncle'. *Uncle* Billy.

He was a kiddie-fiddler. That's what he did to me and my sister Clare. Fiddle. Get each of us on our own upstairs, make sure no one else was around to see. Push us on a bed, tickle us. Try and kiss us. Tickle us down... He'd put his whole body on top of you and... I was little. I was six when it started; Clare was nine. His perfect age.

You know, I've thought about this a lot and... I think he married Auntie Maggie because he knew she had two little kids in her life.

Beat.

That's not sexy is it?

She walks off. The sound of throwing up. MANNY disappears.

CLARE's flat. Music on low. CLARE's busy – doing some kind of task. A distraction from what she's saying.

CLARE. Uncle Billy had always liked this old rock-and-roll singer – Billy Fury. 'I Will' was his favourite song. Played it all the time.

I told Auntie Maggie I didn't like the way Uncle Billy kissed me. She just told me to keep my teeth together.

One day, I was ten, he had me on the bed and I. I said if he kept doing it, I'd tell Mum and Dad. And he stopped. Just like that. Never did it again. I told Ange to do the same. And she said that he stopped it with her too.

Which I thought was true.

I really thought that was true.

Only… eight years ago, Ange and me got blind drunk with Mum. And Ange just started on her, asked Mum if she'd known about Uncle Billy? Mum said she didn't know anything about it.

When I told Auntie Maggie she said that he was just being friendly. That I'd got it wrong. So, I realised it was up to me. To defend myself.

Beat.

And I thought that when I told Ange what to do, I thought I'd defended her too. I thought I'd saved us, but.

But eight years ago… I found out Uncle Billy carried on with Ange for another four years, until she was eleven. And she hadn't told me. Until then.

I thought it had stopped.

I really thought it had stopped.

She doesn't like to talk about it. We've never discussed it. Not properly. She's never said what happened. So, I… I imagine the worst.

And eight years ago, I stopped breathing. I haven't breathed since. I just pretend to.

JOSIE *at her promontory.*

JOSIE. When I was thirteen, I got ninety-six per cent in my maths exam. That's pretty amazing, right? But afterwards, in class, we were going through the papers looking at where we'd lost marks when I saw… I saw there were four points that hadn't been added in on my paper. I had one hundred per cent.

I asked my teacher if he'd change the mark on my report. He said he couldn't, not once it was written. He said I knew what I had, he knew what I had, that was enough. But that wasn't fair. I wanted it in black and white. I wanted proof. I asked my dad to talk to the teacher, but he couldn't be bothered, and I thought…

I thought what's the point? What's the point of even trying?
Who cares?

So, I didn't bother after that.

GRAHAM *stands overlooking the Thames. This is different
to* JOSIE*'s place.*

GRAHAM. A common place for river-based suicides this.
Doesn't look that deep. But it's the current.

I thought I'd come and take a look.

I want to talk to my passengers, the ones like me, the lonely
ones but it's like a patchy signal. Just as you start getting
somewhere, the journey's ended.

You lose the connection.

The lights start going out until all that's left is moonshine.

Oh.

Power cut.

CLARE*'s flat.* CLARE *alone in the darkness. Uses her
phone torch as light.*

It's silent. CLARE *uses her phone to play some music, it's
tinny. Dies. The light too.*

CLARE. Shit.

It's dim. Barely any light. CLARE *starts singing to herself,
quietly. She gets under her duvet. Her singing stops.*

We hear the sound of amplified breathing.

CLARE *sits up. It stops.*

Repeats.

It gets louder. Reaches a crescendo. CLARE *curls up, tries
to protect herself.*

Woodside Hospice. ANGE *finds herself in the same position as* CLARE. *She doesn't know why. She unfurls*.

Flashback: BEX *approaches her.*

ANGE. I missed the fundraiser! I'm sorry! Shit.

BEX. It doesn't matter. We raised nine hundred quid. Everyone loved it. Only three kids threw up on the bouncy castle and one case of sunstroke, so... Y'know, result.

I wanted to give you the money in person.

She hands the cheque over.

Everyone had a lovely day. Lovely weather. Blue skies. It was a laugh.

Yeah, there was a lot of laughter.

ANGE. Sounds brilliant.

BEX. It's come back.

It's everywhere. But it's not going to get me. It's the monster coming back just before I get it again.

She starts crying.

I told myself I wouldn't cry.

ANGE. Tell yourself to shut up, you can totally cry.

BEX. I just feel so... Angry.

ANGE. You're allowed to get angry.

BEX. I don't want my family to see me like this. I mean... I did *everything*.

ANGE. What do you want to do? Do you want to come back to day clinic?

BEX. Yeah. I think I'd like that.

I needed that. Feel better now it's out.

She starts.

Oh yeah! I wanted to tell you. I had this dream about my boys.

There was Bradley and Luke. Only they were older. And they weren't talking. I knew they hadn't talked in months. My fella was sat watching telly and it was like he didn't care. I shouted at him. Tried to talk to Bradley, tried talking to Luke, but no one could hear me. And then I realised. I wasn't there. I woke up, had this like this panic attack.

It's a classic anxiety dream, right? Significant. Have you spoken to your sister yet?

ANGE. Yeah. It's fine, it's all fine.

No, I haven't. Not yet.

BEX. Talk to her.

BEX *disappears. Present day.* GRAHAM *stands at the entrance to the hospice. He sees* ANGE *watching him, he backs away.*

GRAHAM. I'll wait outside.

The Butcher's Slab. CLARE *stumbles into the space, half-drunk.*

CLARE. I've just called Clive a pervert at work. He'd been hugging again. Being 'friendly'. I said it wasn't professional. I went outside my office. Spoke to everyone. Told the women to watch out for Clive, because Clive was a pervert.

Someone sniggered and I… See, I'm off the wagon and I'm not sleeping and I…

I lost it. Said they needed to grow up, stop acting like they're back at school, bitching behind the bike sheds. Leaving people out. I told them I saw their Instagram posts. The ones of them paintballing and having a pub lunch at the weekend. Did anyone bother to ask me if I'd like to go paintballing? No. I told them they were all fuckers!

I got quite angry. Then my boss, Phil, called me into his office.

He said I smelt of alcohol. I may have had a vodka at lunch but only one. I explained that I hadn't slept. I was a little under the weather. Phil said I obviously needed some time off. Pull myself together. Go home. I said –

I don't want to go home, Phil. I want to stay here.

He said I wasn't in any state to do my job. That there was no shame in asking for help. It made me laugh. That's what I'm meant to say. I think he found it a bit inappropriate.

CLARE *laughs. Can't stop. But it turns into something painful. A cry for help.*

King's Cross Station. The sound of a busy train station. MANNY *sits, nervous, at a table with two coffees. He's waiting for someone.*

JOSIE *enters, wears a jacket over a yellow shirt with black polka dots, like the one* BEX *wears.* MANNY *stands.*

JOSIE. I've been worried sick. You're not answering my calls. My texts.

MANNY. Sit down, Mum.

JOSIE. What's happened? Where are you staying?

MANNY. Stop, please stop. There's no easy way to say this, so I'm just going to say it.

JOSIE. Have you failed the year? Have you got someone pregnant? Is it drugs? Oh my God, my son's on drugs.

MANNY. Mum, with the greatest respect will you please shut up. Please.

If JOSIE*'s looks could kill,* MANNY *would be dead right now.*

Please. Please, Mum.

Beat.

You know how I found it tough when I started at Cambridge...

JOSIE. Course. We spoke nearly every day.

MANNY. Yeah. It took a long time, but I got through it. Now being there feels almost normal. I mean I still have imposter syndrome but everyone there has that.

JOSIE. You're not an imposter, you –

MANNY. I know. I know I'm not, that's why I said imposter *syndrome*. Will you. Will you please just listen? You've got to let me say this.

It was hard at first, lonely. But I got used to it. And most people got used to me. I got mates. The course is great. I mean it's relentless, but it's good, only... And this is why I'm saying all this, cos it's not for any of those reasons but. I don't want to be there any more, at Cambridge.

I've don't think I ever wanted to be.

I did it because you wanted me to. And now, I feel trapped. Like it's not my life. Like I'm living the life you wanted to live.

I can't do it any more. I feel like... Like I'm suffocating. You suffocate me, Mum.

JOSIE. That why you brought me here, in front of people, so I wouldn't make a scene? Don't think that'll stop me.

MANNY. Nothing will stop you. I do know you. I brought you here because I'm between shifts.

JOSIE. This is them. The other students, your lecturers, the supervisors. Making you feel you're not good enough. That you're different. Not clever enough. You're just scared.

MANNY. I'm *not* scared. I know I'm clever enough, Mum. I know I can do it. You're not listening.

JOSIE. Yeah, well you're not making sense. Seriously, are you on drugs?

MANNY (*for fuck's sake*). Stop it! Will you just.

You have two of these – (*Indicates ears.*) and one of this – (*Indicates mouth.*) for a reason. If you don't start listening,

I'm walking away. Because this ain't easy. Having this conversation with you.

JOSIE *raises an eyebrow – 'okay'*.

I never had a choice about it. Cambridge. You never gave me a choice. You mapped out my whole life for me since I was twelve. I tried to get out of it. But then Granddad got ill and all I wanted was to make you happy. So, I followed the map.

I'm going to finish my degree somewhere else. It'll be my choice.

Beat.

JOSIE. You finished? Am I allowed to speak now? You do this and you're making the biggest mistake of your life. You're throwing it all away. You've been there two years, you're doing well. It's Cambridge! One of the best universities in the world. You get a degree there and you can walk into anywhere, any job. It's the golden ticket. You don't just chuck the golden ticket in the bin cos you're fed up of holding it. You're giving up the moment it gets tough.

MANNY. I'm in my *second* year, I'm not walking away cos it's tough. The thing to get, Mum, the thing right – it's not the golden ticket. You have no idea what it's like, how it works. You've read some brochures, seen a load of photos online.

JOSIE. I know what it's like! I could have gone there!

MANNY. But you didn't. And if you had, do you think you would have survived? Cos I don't.

You think once you're in, that's it – your life's made. But you get there and see, close up, how life really works. It's not a level playing field and never has been. The entitlement, the privilege it's… People who think a hundred pounds is loose change. They've already got their jobs, their internships. They had them before they started. The connections, the networks, the friend of Mummy and Daddy's. They don't share that shit; they keep it to themselves. For people like them.

They like me, I'm easy-going, I'm friendly… I have to be. Because every time I go to a college that isn't Trinity, I'm asked why I'm there, who I'm there to see. I nearly missed a supervision because the porters wouldn't let me in. And they'd just let in four white boys who – (*Does an RP accent.*) talk like this. Hi, man, I've got my supervision here.

Me, nah. My supervisor had to come down and get them to let me in. If I change my voice, put on an accent, it's fine. People think I'm one of them.

But I don't want to change myself. Why should I?

MANNY *is intensely vulnerable. Emotional.*

Cambridge wasn't about me. It was about you. It always was. And I can't do it any more. Because that's why I get anxious. And every time I see you, the more it comes back. That anxiety. And there's nothing to split your focus. No Granddad or Queenie. It's all me. And I'm suffocating, Mum, It's suffocating me...

He goes toward JOSIE, *to hold her, but she steps back.*

JOSIE. You spoilt, ungrateful...

She walks away, doesn't look at him.

London street. JOSIE *stands by herself.*

I walked away. Didn't stop till I reached my place by the river. My special place. But it was full of people. Families. Mothers and sons. Felt like I was being poked all over. Poke.

I can't get a Tube. It's too packed. All those people. I can't get the bus. I want to be by myself. You can never be alone in London.

I just want to go home.

JOSIE *puts her arm out.*

GRAHAM. Where to?

JOSIE. Peckham High Street.

JOSIE sits in the back, takes off her jacket. GRAHAM sees her yellow shirt with the black polka dots. She can see him looking in the mirror. Makes her uncomfortable.

GRAHAM. That's a nice –

JOSIE. I've had a pig of a day. I don't want to talk.

GRAHAM. Right. Fine. You're the boss.

He turns the radio on.

Like Radio 2?

JOSIE. No.

GRAHAM. Classic FM?

JOSIE. No.

GRAHAM. Talk radio?

JOSIE. What do you think?

He turns the radio off. They travel in silence.

GRAHAM. She didn't say one word to me. Not one word.

I don't like silence.

Your mind can go anywhere.

The more silent she is, the more I start to think that maybe I'm not really here.

JOSIE. Take the next left, I'm off here.

And now the second road on the right.

JOSIE *sniffs. Sniffs again.*

What's that? That's burning. Something's wrong with your engine.

GRAHAM. Y'what?

JOSIE. Burning. I smell burning inside the cab. Pull over. Can't you smell that?

They stop.

GRAHAM. I can't smell anything.

JOSIE. Like. Like something electrical, like the wires are about to catch fire.

Get out. We need to get out.

GRAHAM *and* JOSIE *get out.*

Oh, it's gone.

It's not there any more. Did you smell it?

GRAHAM. I didn't smell anything.

JOSIE. Start the engine again.

He does.

Turn it off! That's weird. Nothing there now.

GRAHAM. Maybe it was sommat we drove past?

JOSIE. No, the windows were done up. It was in the cab. It's just.

Weird.

She sees GRAHAM *look at her strangely.*

What?

GRAHAM. It's just. I like your blouse. My wife had it. I wanted to say it looked nice.

JOSIE. Your wife had it? What did she do? Lose it? Donate it to a charity shop?

GRAHAM. She died. My wife, she died.

JOSIE. Oh.

I'm sorry. When?

GRAHAM. Just a few months ago. Cancer. After she had our youngest.

JOSIE. How many kids have you got?

GRAHAM. Two. Two sons.

JOSIE. How are you coping?

GRAHAM. Oh, fine. We're good.

JOSIE. How are you really coping?

   GRAHAM *breaks down*.

GRAHAM. Not good. The boys are just. They need me to be strong. To keep it together. To keep normal. And I feel like I want to. I don't know... I feel *everything*.

   I should go, you don't want to hear this.

JOSIE. Yes, I do.

   You're coming in, having a cup of tea and we're gonna talk. No arguments.

   JOSIE*'s flat*. JOSIE *makes tea. Her back to* GRAHAM *who sits at the table, emotional*.

   I know what you're going through, Graham. My mum got cancer when she was pregnant with me. Twenty-three months later, she died. And my dad. He didn't cope.

   I understand.

   Do you have sugar?

   GRAHAM*'s moved, walks over towards* JOSIE. *He goes to hug her. They disappear*.

   CLARE*'s flat. Just a corner of it*. CLARE *alone*.

CLARE. The GP said my meds would kick in any day. That I'd be back to normal. I'm sleeping fine again. I'm sleeping all the time. No dreams, just blackness.

   I didn't tell my GP about the breathing. Well, there have to be some things a girl keeps to herself.

   Steve came around and picked the rest of his stuff up. He was nice. Sweet. Kind. I wish he'd been horrible. I wish he'd let me be angry at him. Kindness was...

   It was brutal.

JOSIE*'s flat*. JOSIE *and* GRAHAM *sit at a table, with cups of tea.*

GRAHAM. I'm sorry, Josie, about… Sorry. I don't know what I was thinking.

JOSIE. Lucky I didn't punch you.

You don't have to keep apologising.

You can't bottle it all up. That's what my dad did.

You need to leave your boys for a while. Be angry. Be upset. Let it out. Everything. All the emotions. They're okay with their Auntie Linda.

And it must be confusing for them, you not being there. Working all hours. Day and night. This way you give them structure. They'll know they're not seeing you for a bit, but after that, well. Then you'll be back. Properly back.

GRAHAM. But if I go… I don't want them to think I don't love them.

JOSIE. Tell them you love them. Tell them all the time. Write to them. Call. Skype. This is the most loving thing you can do for them. Taking yourself away to heal.

See, my dad never did that. Never healed. He never said he loved me. Not once. Men didn't, his generation. And that hurt. It physically hurt.

He wouldn't even look at me. Even when I was small. I knew it was because he couldn't forgive me for me being born and Mum dying. He was angry all the time. He couldn't cope with his feelings. He had so many and he didn't know what to do with any of them.

Must've died about the same time as your Bex.

She finds herself crying.

Oh…

GRAHAM. God, I've set you off, now. Sorry.

JOSIE. First time I've done that. Cry for Dad. I cried for my dog, Queenie. Cried every night for months. Still do. But never for him.

I think now – saying it to you – it's because… there's all this hurt. All this… Upset and I can't do anything with it. There's nowhere for it to go, because he's not here.

Beat.

I got a hundred per cent in an exam for him. I wanted him to notice me. To be proud.

She pulls herself together.

I don't normally do this. I never do this.

Y'know, I think your wife made us meet.

GRAHAM. Wouldn't surprise me. She was always banging on about that – the universe…

GRAHAM*'s phone alarm goes off, he stands.*

Need to pick the kids up. Better go. Thank you. I appreciate it. You taking the time.

JOSIE *waves it away, he sees her box of tapes from* MANNY.

Don't often see those – tapes.

JOSIE. My son gave them to me. Conversations he had with my dad when he was younger. Just talking.

GRAHAM. Are they interesting?

JOSIE. Don't know, I haven't listened. I haven't got a tape player.

GRAHAM. What about that?

He indicates the hi-fi.

JOSIE. Doesn't work. No lead.

Flashback: Woodside Hospice. BEX is a hospital bed. She's dying. Unhooked machines nearby. GRAHAM with her, he checks his phone.

GRAHAM. The boys are at Linda's.

BEX. It's good that we've said goodbye.

GRAHAM. Yeah.

BEX winces.

D'you need some more pain relief?

BEX. Nah, I'm already flying. Not been this high since I was seventeen. How much longer will it take?

GRAHAM. She said not long now.

BEX. Make sure the kids always stay friends. Never go to bed on an argument.

GRAHAM. Course. Don't you worry about anything, you.

BEX. Will you give them the memory boxes? Ange has got them, I think.

GRAHAM. I've got them. They're safe at home.

BEX. Good.

Now. And this is very important.

GRAHAM. Yes, love.

BEX. Promise me you and the boys will always eat something green every day. No eating shit just cos I've gone. And tell the boys I'm not talking about bogeys. If you don't eat your greens, I'll come back and bloody haunt you!

GRAHAM. Yes, please.

Time moves forward. BEX now at the very end.

BEX. I'm ready.

I don't want to fight it any more.

Haven't the energy.

I love you.

Beat.

GRAHAM. I love you too.

She closes her eyes. Her hand gets slack.

Her breathing becomes laboured, rattles. Is this it?

Bex…? Bex?

BEX *opens her eyes.*

BEX. Gah. Takes longer than you'd think.

GRAHAM can't help laughing and, in that moment, BEX dies.

GRAHAM stays still as ANGE enters. GRAHAM watches as BEX is taken away in her bed. Away from him. He's a solitary figure on stage. GRAHAM stands.

Present day. GRAHAM puts on a jacket. ANGE approaches him.

GRAHAM. I'm picking up Bernard Birch.

ANGE. I think he's ready for you. How are the kids?

GRAHAM walks towards her. It's the first time he's not backed out of there.

GRAHAM. We'll get there.

I'm going away. Need some time on my own. Breathing space.

Beat.

Is it all okay with your sister, now?

ANGE. Oh yes, it's all fine. Something and nothing. Sorted it all out. It's all…

GRAHAM disappears. ANGE feels herself twist.

CLARE's flat. CLARE echoes ANGE's movement. She unfolds, freaked out. WTF?

Fix-U-Fast Autos. JOSIE at the front desk, reading a magazine. The ting of a bell as someone enters. JOSIE doesn't look up. GRAHAM enters.

JOSIE. We're closed. Oh…

GRAHAM. It's just me. I'm not stalking you. Honest. It's just that you said you worked here. And I wanted to give you something. To say thank you.

He hands over a plastic bag. JOSIE looks inside and pulls out a lead.

It's for your hi-fi. It's a standard power lead – should fit. So you can listen to your dad's tapes. It'll make it work.

JOSIE, thrown. Considers the lead, thoughtful. GRAHAM exits.

JOSIE. Thank you.

But he's gone.

JOSIE looks at the framed newspaper cutting of MANNY. Pulls it down. Hears the sound of a dog panting, the rattle of a dog collar. She looks down, then back at the photo. It hits her.

King's Cross Station. JOSIE waits. She's there first this time.

MANNY arrives. He's wary, defensive.

Hey.

MANNY. Hey.

JOSIE. Y'know, when Queenie was ill, one of my friends said it was better to have her put down two weeks too early, than a day too late. Do you remember? It was the hardest decision I've ever made. But I had to do right by her.

MANNY. Is this your way of telling me you're thinking of having me put down?

JOSIE. No! Course not. I'm talking about what's right for you.

MANNY. I know. That was a joke.

JOSIE. I'm not happy about you leaving Cambridge. I think you're making a big mistake. Huge. But... go where you want, do what you want. Just be happy.

MANNY. Okay what have you done with my mum? Because right now, I'm fucking worried.

JOSIE. Oi, language!

MANNY. Ah, she's back.

They look at each other for the longest time. Like it's the first time they've seen each other.

I'm sorry.

JOSIE. No, no. You've got nothing to be sorry about. It's me that's the miserable old cow. I'm so proud of you, baby. You do what's right for you.

MANNY *draws her in close for a hug. Goes to pull away but* JOSIE *keeps hold of him.*

Know what I read the other day? That if you hug for longer than twenty seconds you create pheromones. Feel-good pheromones.

MANNY. That right?

JOSIE. We can try it. Science experiment.

MANNY *gives in to the hug then...*

MANNY. That's got to be twenty seconds.

JOSIE *keeps hugging.*

JOSIE. Five more...

GRAHAM *stands at* JOSIE'*s promontory. Looks at the*
Thames. Alone.

GRAHAM. This was frozen once. People walked from one side
of the Thames to the other.

I saw it on *Doctor Who*. Googled it. It was all true. Well,
apart from that alien living underneath it. Obviously.

He looks back out to the river.

Someone jumped from here too last week. By the time they
fished his body out, it was quarter of a mile down the river.

GRAHAM *looks down at the river.*

ANGE'*s home*. ANGE *suddenly finds herself contorting.*
What…? She contorts again.

CLARE'*s flat.* CLARE *in bed. She's making the same*
movements, she's sobbing.

ANGE *finds herself sobbing too. For a moment we see both*
sisters. ANGE *disappears and we're left with* CLARE *and*
the sound of breathing. We're inside CLARE'*s nightmare.*

She dreams of faceless men who try to embrace her. They
hide in the shadows. She tries to hide inside the wardrobe,
but a faceless man steps out of it. Arms reach for her. As they
nearly touch her, the sound of a door banging. It's like in
horror films.

It dissolves into an entry phone buzzing. Wakes CLARE.
It buzzes again. CLARE *goes to the entry phone. Scared.*

CLARE. Hello? Who's there?

She buzzes them in. Uses the time to straighten herself up.
Drink some water. She grabs a bottle of wine. Pours a glass
as there's a knock at the door. She opens it to reveal ANGE.

What's happened? What's wrong?

ANGE. Nothing's wrong. Can I come in?

CLARE *lets her in.*

Steve not here?

CLARE. No.

ANGE. I just had a really weird thing happen. And I just. I felt I should see you.

CLARE. Well, it's been a while.

Beat.

Work's been busy and...

She sips wine. Makes ANGE *uncomfortable.*

ANGE. You're drinking?

CLARE. Do you want one?

ANGE. No, thanks. How many have you had?

CLARE. This is my first. You woke me up, I was in bed.

ANGE. Maybe you should have water first?

CLARE. I've had some water.

CLARE *takes another sip of wine.*

ANGE. Do you have to drink?

CLARE. I'm not getting drunk. God, it's one drink.

ANGE. Only. It's not very.

You never call me and then you call me six times in the middle of the night. I kept asking you to phone back later but you wouldn't stop calling. And I was on duty, I couldn't turn my phone off. You weren't very nice.

CLARE. I can't remember. I was drunk, I hadn't eaten. Whatever I said, I didn't mean it.

ANGE. I think we quite often speak the truth when we're drunk.

CLARE *rolls her eyes*.

So, where is Steve?

CLARE. I haven't got a fucking clue.

ANGE. Has he… Has he left?

CLARE. Bingo.

ANGE. He's at bingo?

CLARE. Why the fuck would he be at bingo? He's gone. Left. I don't know where he is and I don't care. I'm better off without him. We weren't compatible.

ANGE. I liked him.

CLARE. Yeah, well he thinks you're great. Said he found it hard to believe we were related. That it was like you'd been taken from another family and got put in ours by mistake.

ANGE. Why didn't you tell me?

CLARE. Do you want me to phone you up and tell you every compliment?

ANGE. I wasn't talking about that. Why did he leave? Was there someone else?

CLARE. No, no, it was just me.

ANGE. Do you want to talk about it?

CLARE. Fuck no.

She hears a creak.

ANGE. You look awful.

CLARE. Thanks, I was feeling better.

Beat.

ANGE. Listen, Clare…

CLARE. Don't. Don't put on that voice. That 'St Angela' voice. *Clare…* I'm not one of your patients. Don't therapy me. Don't make it all about me.

ANGE. You want me to just sit here in silence?

CLARE. I didn't ask you to come round.

ANGE. No, I came round, because I thought there was something wrong.

She reaches out to her sister, tries to touch her. CLARE *starts getting upset.*

CLARE. I don't want your kindness! I don't want you to be nice. I don't want you to be understanding. Why are you always so fucking calm?

ANGE. What's happened? Is it Steve? Is it work? Is it…

CLARE. I've been signed off.

She starts crying. Doesn't want ANGE *to see.*

ANGE. Oh, Clare. Why? Come here…

She goes to hug CLARE, *but* CLARE *steps back.*

CLARE. Don't. I'll spill my wine.

ANGE. Fuck the wine.

CLARE. It's the carpet! It's an expensive carpet!

ANGE. Jesus. Fine. This is why, I…

What are you signed off with?

Shit… Is Clare dying?

Are you ill?

Clare, will you talk to me? Are you ill?

CLARE. I just. I had a bit of a. Bit of a breakdown. I wasn't sleeping. I'm on antidepressants now, so that's all fine.

Look, I've stopped crying. I don't want to be upset.

Let's forget about it. Have a drink, have some fun.

CLARE pours ANGE *a glass of wine,* ANGE *can feel upset welling up inside her. Tries to cover.*

ANGE. How much are you drinking?

CLARE. Oh, for God's sake. It doesn't matter. I don't have work to go into!

ANGE. Yes, but if you're on antidepressants –

CLARE. I've checked. They're fine. I can drink with them. Cheers!

She downs her wine.

ANGE. Maybe you should take it easy.

It makes you a bit...

CLARE *pours herself another glass of wine.*

I find it difficult.

CLARE. You find *me* difficult.

ANGE. I... I can't talk to you when you're like this.

You always want an argument –

CLARE. Oh, fuck off. That's just bollocks –

ANGE. I don't want to argue with you.

CLARE. You're just oversensitive because you work with dying people! Why did you even come over? To lecture me? Tell me how to be a better person? Tell me what I've done wrong? To show me how fucking calm you are? All the fucking time!

ANGE. I can't do this. I'll come back another day.

CLARE. Go on then.

ANGE. Why are you being like this?

CLARE. Like what?

ANGE. Like this.

CLARE *shrugs. Pours more wine.*

The longest beat.

You were angry with me on the phone. Really angry.

I know you're angry with me.

CLARE *laughs suddenly. Inappropriately. It makes her cry.*

ANGE *feels her eyes smart with tears. This is what she's terrified to say. Her biggest fear.*

I know you think I'm weak. Because I let it go on. Because I didn't tell him to stop like you told me to. That you blame me.

This pierces CLARE*'s heart. Devastates her.*

CLARE. I blame you? You think that's why I'm angry?

ANGE. You've barely talked to me for eight years. Just birthdays and Christmases and that's it.

CLARE *shakes her head. The sound of breathing low.*

CLARE. No.

No.

No, no, no, no…

I…

ANGE. I… I understand, it's okay.

CLARE. No. I…

The breathing gets louder. ANGE *oblivious to it.* CLARE *can hear it.*

I… I… I never protected you.

I should've said something. Told someone. I could have stopped it. I should have told him to leave you alone. But I left you to do it on your own. You were tiny.

ANGE. And you were ten.

CLARE. Exactly. *Three* years older. I'm the *oldest* sister.

ANGE. No, I mean you were a child too. Look at me, Clare. You were a little kid.

The sound of breathing.

CLARE. You never said what happened. I mean I know you
said you've dealt with it.

ANGE. I have. I don't want it in my present, that's all. I've
talked about it. I've had counselling.

CLARE. But the thing is… we've never talked about it. And I.

I don't know what happened to you. And I know you don't
want to talk about it, but I don't know. And I imagine the
worst. And… Did he… Did he…

ANGE. He didn't. He didn't rape me. He didn't. It was never
anything like that.

It was kissing and tickling and molesting. That's what it was
– molesting. Till he asked me to touch him and. I told him to
stop right away. I said I'd tell you. And he did. Stop. He
never did it again.

The sound of breathing starts to retreat. For the first time,
CLARE *feels like she can breathe.*

I felt. I felt ashamed I hadn't said it before. When you told
me to.

CLARE. It was my fault.

ANGE. No! No. If we're blaming anyone, we're blaming Uncle
Billy. And Auntie Maggie. And Mum and Dad, because we
could never tell them. We were children. We should never
have had to deal with that shit.

Beat.

CLARE. I thought you hated me.

ANGE. Well, I don't like you sometimes.

You're really fucking argumentative.

And critical about everything.

Self-obsessed.

You're very dominating.

And your flat's much nicer than mine.

But I don't hate you. Hate's a very strong word.

The sound of breathing comes back. The shadows... CLARE *spies them.*

I love you too, you silly cow. I always looked up to you. Still do.

Beat.

And anyway, you did protect me, you just didn't know. I used to creep into your room when we were little. Climb into your spare bed. I didn't like sleeping on my own. I always left before you woke up. You never saw me. I slept there almost every night.

I felt safe in your room. Just wanted to be with you.

The shadows and sound of breathing disappear instantly.

CLARE. It was you. It was your breathing I heard.

Fuck. Fuck.

CLARE *laughs, can't stop.*

The two sisters face each other. Take each other in as if for the first time. They look lighter.

They hug. A fierce hug. A hug that's longed to be had. Disappear.

GRAHAM *finishes packing a suitcase. He pulls out the yellow shirt with black polka dots from the wardrobe. Inhales it, emotional.*

He pulls himself together. Puts the shirt away. Carries his suitcase to a doorway.

GRAHAM. Who's going to give their old dad a hug before he goes?

He pretends to be a bear as he disappears from view. We hear childish squeals of laughter.

JOSIE's flat. MANNY puts in the lead GRAHAM gave
JOSIE. She considers the box of tapes.

JOSIE. Does it work?

He switches it on at the hi-fi.

MANNY. Yes!

JOSIE. Which tape is first? There's so many. I don't know
where to start. Which one to –

MANNY. Maybe the one with the sticker on that says: 'listen to
this one first'?

He goes through the box.

I've been thinking. I might go back to Cambridge. Might.

JOSIE. Yeah?

She nods, doesn't push it.

He gives her a tape. She puts it in. She turns the volume up.
Presses play.

We hear her dad – he sounds old – and a young teenage
MANNY, *his voice unbroken.*

DAD'S VOICE. This was when your mum was three.

MANNY. I was showing him photos and he was talking about
them.

DAD'S VOICE. She was clever even then. Reading at three.
That's who you got your brains from. She's a very clever
woman, your mother.

MANNY *watches his mum. Gives her some space.*

The moment she was born, I fell in love with her. She was
the spitting image of your grandmother.

I loved her so much, I was worried I'd squeeze her too tight
and break her.

YOUNG MANNY'S VOICE. You should tell her you love her,
Granddad.

DAD'S VOICE. Oh, I don't need to do that. She knows I love her. I don't have to tell her. She knows how I feel. Show me another photo.

JOSIE *presses pause. Rewinds the tape.*

She knows I love her. I don't have to tell her. She knows how I feel.

JOSIE *rewinds the tape again.*

She knows I love her.

JOSIE *and* MANNY *disappear.*

CLARE*'s flat.* ANGE *makes ready to go.* CLARE *in organisation mode.*

CLARE. I want us to see each other regularly. Come for dinner every week. We'll make a thing of it. You can stay. We could do something together. Maybe a class?

ANGE. Maybe.

But let's take it slow.

I think.

I think we should be careful with each other. Gentle. Like we would with a stranger. Give each other space.

CLARE. But.

Right. Yeah, okay.

Okay.

As ANGE *leaves, they brush hands.* ANGE *disappears.*

CLARE *takes in her room. Breathes. We hear the slight tinny sound of a radio playing somewhere in the flat.* CLARE *goes and finds it. Turns it off. Stands still in the silence.*

Blackout.

The End.

A Nick Hern Book

I Think We Are Alone first published as a paperback original in Great Britain in 2020 by Nick Hern Books Limited, The Glasshouse, 49a Goldhawk Road, London W12 8QP, in association with Frantic Assembly, Theatre Royal Plymouth and Curve Theatre, Leicester

I Think We Are Alone copyright © 2020 Sally Abbott

Sally Abbott has asserted her right to be identified as the author of this work

Cover image: Model: Ebony Molina; Photography: Perou; Design: Feast

Designed and typeset by Nick Hern Books, London
Printed in Great Britain by CPI Group (Ltd)

A CIP catalogue record for this book is available from the British Library

ISBN   978 1 84842 934 5

www.nickhernbooks.co.uk

facebook.com/nickhernbooks

twitter.com/nickhernbooks